You'll Get Out Of It When You Learn To Love It

Rachel Wortman

First edition

For the purspose of this publication we have chosen not to capitalize satan and all related names. We do not wish to acknowledge him, even to the point of violating grammatical rules.

ISBN 978-1-7340994-0-9

DEDICATION

To my precious Kingston Sparrow Wortman.
Without your brief life I would not have been
forced to face the pain I was so adamant to hide. I
think of you often. I miss you constantly. I am so
jealous that you get to live all your days in heaven.
Until we meet again...

ACKNOWLEDGEMENTS

TO MY HUSBAND...

Grant, you have been my biggest champion in this life. Thank you for your relentless support, your endless reminders that God called me to write this book, and your passion to see me thrive. I love you.

TO MY KIDS...

Eli, Callie, Jack, & Grace! I love being your mom! You all bring me so much joy. Thank you for keeping me humble, reminding me I'm not perfect, and enjoying tv and Disney as much as I do.

TO DR. JENNA GOGGINS...

I am not sure this book would have made it this far without your prayers, support, and advice. Your editing made this project soar. Thank you for being such a powerful force of good in my life!

TO MY GURIAN FAM...

Mom, Dad, David, and Kristina I love you all. Thank you for encouraging me to stick with it, humoring all my crazy ideas, and being some of my favorite people ever.

TO GRAHAM COOKE...

Although I only met you once it was a conversation that changed me forever. Thank you for your obedience to speak truth to me around my table that day. Your words pointed me towards a breakthrough in Jesus I desperately needed. Your teachings have elevated my understanding of God and have been a consistent source of help in my life.

TO MY GOD...

Last on this list but certainly not least in my heart. There will never be enough words to say how much I love you. You really did rescue me from my strong enemy. You delivered me and brought me into a wide space to thrive. I owe you everything. You have my continual yes.

TABLE OF CONTENTS

INTRODUCTION..11
1. THE WORST OF TIMES....................................15
2. THE BEST OF TIMES...29
3. TANGIBLE EXPERIENCE..................................41
4. WRESTLE MANIA..53
5. YOUR SECRET WEAPON...................................65
6. SPIRITUAL WARFARE.......................................79
7. WHERE DID THAT COME FROM?...............91
8. HE CALLED IT LOVE......................................103
9. YOUR GREATEST BATTLE............................115
10. HIDING IN PLAIN SIGHT............................129
11. UNFAIR ADVANTAGE...................................141
12. PERMISSION TO THRIVE............................153

ABOUT THE AUTHOR.......................................167
FREEBIES..171

INTRODUCTION

One crisp autumn evening I was driving home at dusk and heard the Holy Spirit whisper an idea into my heart. He said, "*You should write a book about how you found breakthrough so others can do the same.*" The idea was equally as thrilling as it was daunting. Millions of doubts flooded my mind as I tried to talk myself out of it. How would I find the time with my kids being so young? What would I even say? How much is too much to share? And yet, I couldn't shake the sense that God had called me to do it.

A few evenings later I showed up to Starbucks (my least favorite place on earth) with my laptop in hand ready to try and write a book. I fumbled around with some words for an hour or so and left feeling pretty defeated. As I made the journey home I prayed a simple prayer. *"God, if you are calling me to this then you have something in mind. If you will write this book through me I will give you my hands, my time, and whatever else is needed to make this happen."*

That was 5 years ago. Since then I have written and re-written the words on these pages. I have had my fair share of doubts that it was God telling me to write this book. I have had to set it down and walk away for long periods of time. But I kept coming back because I know for certain the words in this book are words of life. They are words of breakthrough. They are keys to freedom. I need them and I suspect you do too.

Rest assured these words are not just random thoughts or poetic fluff. They are the very tools I have used to step into a life better than I could have dreamed of. They are words that have wrecked and re-shaped my life. I have preached them. I have lived them. I have seen them transform the lives of those around me. I am praying they do the same for you.

You are about to get up close and personal to my story. The good, the bad, the ugly, and the down right embarrassing. Yet weirdly, I am ok with it because I know there is power in the testimony. I need you to know that if God has done it for me He can do it for you. Let my testimony be a prophetic word of promise. The abundant life is truly available for you. You can learn to thrive in Jesus. You will get out of whatever you are stuck in because He is just that good.

As I came to the end of the writing and publishing journey I felt another whisper from Holy Spirit to my heart. This time it was about getting these words into the hands of some of the people who need them the most. So we have decided to do something a little zany!

For every copy of this book that is sold we will be giving one to someone in a life repair and recovery situation. We have partnered with some prison ministries, rehab facilities for traffic victims, and recovery houses to give free copies to people who are ready to discover all that God has for them. That means that you are holding a key for someone else's breakthrough as well as your own as you hold this book. Thank you for helping us make that possible.

One more thing worth mentioning: I love hearing how these stories, tools, and activations help you. If you enjoy what you read in this book I would love it if you would leave a book review on amazon, send me a message on social media, or encourage a friend to get this for themselves too.

Have I mentioned that gifts are my love language yet? Giving gifts it probably in my top 3 things I love about life! That is why I have added some freebies in the back of this book just for you. Be sure to check out that section as well.

Ok, enough about all that. Let's start thriving! I am praying for you as you read this book. I am praying that you will feel near to Holy Spirit as He leads you. I am praying you will find it easy to open your heart and let God in like never before. I am praying you get all the breakthrough you are longing for. I am praying you enjoy the journey of learning to love your life.

Blessings,

Rachel

chapter one

THE WORST OF TIMES

At what point do you go ahead and deem something "the worst"? For me, it happens by comparison. When I look back on my life it is as clear as day that 2011 was the beginning of the worst years of my life. As a 27 year old mother of two young children I had no reason to not like my life. No outward reason, anyway.

Under the surface I was wrestling with big questions. I loved being a stay-at-home mom but I was really starting to resent the limitations I experienced after my second child was born. My husband, Grant, had hit his stride as a youth pastor and he was filling his schedule with all kinds of great opportunities.

Although I was happy for him I was secretly jealous.

Are you ok with me admitting that? I hope so, because in this book I'm going to be brutally honest, and that means you're going to hear the good, the bad, and the ugly. I was carrying the bulk of the family responsibilities and it was taking a toll on me.

I remember one night Grant was leading an outreach with the student ministry at our church and I was at home with our kids. The outing wasn't a good fit for little kids, and after staying back and putting the little ones to bed, I found myself alone and feeing really sad. Grant texted me that 5 youth had come to know Jesus that night. Can you believe that I was almost angry about that? I became so disgusted with myself that my initial response was so bitter and envious. In hindsight, that is the moment I should have reached out for help.

Instead, I started spiraling downward. My thoughts went something like this: How dare you feel this way. Eternity has been changed on this night and you're mad? I quickly shut it down. I knew better. I was a Christian. I was a youth pastor's wife. I was absolutely sure pastors didn't have problems like this.

"Jesus doesn't like my anger," I said to myself as I stuffed the pain down. I turned on the TV to distract myself from myself, once again putting a band-aid over the massive, infected wound lurking in my soul which I refused to acknowledge. How could I? In my mind, acknowledging my wounded heart meant admitting failure. Exposing my unhappiness would send a message to the world that I didn't have what it takes to fulfill my calling as a wife, a mother, or a Christian. Nope. I was not going there!

If only I had known how to handle all my pain and confusion. If I had, this book would not exist. Sadly, this was the beginning of a years long struggle - a very silent struggle. Occasionally I would reach out to a friend or my pastor when things were really bad and dark. But truthfully, I was really afraid of what would happen if I admitted how many questions I was having. Who was God, really? Why didn't He intervene when things got tough? Why didn't things in my life turn out differently? Was I really even called to ministry? I had so many big questions about faith, the Holy Spirit, and so on.

I did not want to ask them because I did not want to jeopardize my place as a leader in the church. I didn't want people to look down on me. I don't think I am alone in that thought process. So many of us are silently struggling - outwardly looking like we have it all together but inwardly trying to navigate big questions.

By the summer of 2011 I was pregnant with my third child. My second child was only 8 months old at the time. The hormones, coupled with the emotional struggles I was already having, meant things got really rough. I took it out on my husband mostly. I was absolutely convinced that if he would just change some things about himself our lives would be so much better. It all came to a boiling point at the end of the summer at our youth camp.

You know that moment in a worship set when the band gets quieter to let everyone have a sweet moment with God? Well, at that exact moment my 4 year old had a complete meltdown. His wailing continuously reverberated around the concrete room of about 400 students and leaders. I couldn't snatch him up fast enough. As I ran out of the meeting room I fell apart. Camp was all packed up because this was the final session. All the cabins were locked up and there was nowhere for me to take him. I started to cry. No, sob.

I eventually made my way back into the meeting room but I was still crying. Grant was still busy running camp and I was losing it. I ducked behind a curtain in the room and tried to pull myself together. All I kept thinking was, "So this is rock bottom? THIS is where you fall apart? In front of all these people?" I was broken. I had nothing left. I was burnt out. I needed help.

A few weeks later Grant and I headed from Oklahoma to Louisiana for a counseling retreat with a counselor that came highly recommended to us. As we drove onto the property I started to cry because I could actually feel God's peace in that place. I was really desperate for help. I needed someone who could wade into the dark waters of my conflicted heart. I was not on the brink of self-harm but I was in the throws of self-hate.

Eddie, the counselor, opened the door and I immediately noticed his waist-length braid. I tried not to judge. I was not doing a good job of it. Within minutes of sitting down he asked me a question. "So...how are you?"

The tears welled up and began to fall out of my eyes as I told my story through Kleenex after Kleenex. I'm a mid-western upper-middle-class girl. By outward appearances I have had very few challenges in life. Inwardly, my heart told a different story. Mine was a story of struggling to love myself, feeling deeply rejected, desperately wanting to be important in this world, and being convinced I never would be. I always felt too tall, too loud, too proper, too black-and-white, too simple, too complex, too aggressive, too much, and yet somehow not enough.

I left that retreat 2 days later a different woman. In session after session we peeled back the layers of misunderstanding, hurt, and heart ache. I was given the tools to process the emotions I was previously so determined to ignore, and I received hope that I could actually find joy in the hard places. That weekend I made a commitment to start learning how to love myself, to work to enjoy the journey of life, to get rid of the ridiculous emotional limitations I had placed on myself, and to give myself permission to thrive.

I wish I could tell you that I went home and miraculously the worst times were over. That all I needed was that moment of love and I was fixed. Ha! The reality was that I did commit to working on my heart but my outward circumstances only grew harder.

FROM BAD TO WORSE

In February of 2012 my third child, Jack, was born. It was a welcome distraction to my healing process. Just four months later I got the surprise of a lifetime and learned I was pregnant again! This would make four babies in five years. At my first doctor's appointment for baby number four they found a tumor on my thyroid and suspected cancer. Just a few months later that surprise-of-a-lifetime baby would surprise me again by moving on to heaven.

The truth is that entire pregnancy just didn't feel right. I thought I was simply overwhelmed at the reality of having four kids in five years. Every appointment I braced myself for the worst only to be told everything was good and healthy. Then, at twenty weeks along, I was scheduled for a routine ultrasound. That morning I was spending time with Jesus and I had a vision of my doctor coming into the exam room and telling me my baby didn't have a heartbeat.

Of course I rebuked that thought and prayed life over my little one. That life would not come. At the appointment everything happened exactly as I had seen in the vision that morning. I was shocked but not surprised. Two days later we delivered our precious, tiny, stillborn baby, a boy we named Kingston Sparrow Wortman. Walking out of the hospital without the baby I came in with was one of the hardest things I have ever done.

The attention turned to my thyroid again and to the threat of cancer. The biopsy came back with no obvious cancer signs but I was advised to have the tumor removed due to its size. So just a few months after saying goodbye to Kingston I had part of my thyroid removed in January of 2013. The surgery initially went well but I wasn't healing correctly. In fact, I kind of felt like I was dying. It turns out I was. I had contracted a serious infection that required a second surgery and a five day hospital stay.

Needless to say, in the span of twenty-two months I went through hell. I mostly bottled it up and kept it close to the vest. I tried to look on the bright side as much as I could but my whole belief system was being ravaged within me. One of the many things I learned through those months is that pain is relative.

You may read my story and think it's not that bad. You may read it and suddenly you think your story is not that bad. The truth is that there is no way to compare one person's pain to another as if there is some imaginary scale we are all being measured with.

The worst times of our lives don't have to be as dramatic as a Lifetime movie to cause us real pain. We have nothing to prove to anyone about why our lives feel hard. If we are struggling then we are struggling. We don't need to wait for someone to validate our pain in order to justify to ourselves that we need to seek help. We don't have to struggle forever, either. I wish I had understood that long before I burnt out.

I think it took me so long to get help because I kept comparing my issues to other people's problems. I waited until I hit rock bottom to even admit to myself that I needed to make some changes. It does not matter how much difficulty you have experienced. What matters is that you find a way through the challenges your life has thrown at you. Too often we try to deny pain because it doesn't meet some invisible standard of culturally accepted crises. We put on a happy face and try to get over whatever is hurting us because on paper it doesn't look like it's all that bad.

This is what was happening to me. I felt alone in my struggle. I was desperately trying to find a way to measure up to what I thought God wanted from me. In some ways, that struggle was significantly more crippling than my health issues. I wrote this book because I am convinced that I am not alone in this struggle. I am convinced that I am not the only person who was unable to navigate the pressures of the Christian life.

The truth is we put so much pressure on ourselves – pressures that God is not actually putting on us. Giving ourselves permission to thrive means giving ourselves permission to discover who we already are in Christ as well as who we are becoming.

The unfulfilled promises, unmet expectations, and disappointments of life often affect us more than we realize. They might seem trivial compared to major traumatic events, yet these disappointments are often the silent killers of our faith. The unchecked thoughts and beliefs lingering in our minds and hearts cause us to question who God is. Soon we are questioning God's faithfulness, wondering if He really is a good Father, and if He loves us as much as that other person over there.

I lived with these questions, and it became my silent struggle. Struggling is not always bad, but I had no clue how to struggle with these things in a way that would lead me to a breakthrough. I was embarrassed that I was even having these thoughts. The shame of admitting my internal reality was too much so I just let them fester until they nearly pushed me away from Jesus altogether.

THE MYSTERY OF FAITH

The problem with these types of questions is the passive aggressive form they typically come in. These questions are not ones we boldly approach the throne of grace with. No, these are questions that we leave in the back of our minds. They are fuel for our suspicions, subtly creating distance between us and our God.

Ironically, God loves a good question. He absolutely jumps at the opportunity to talk with us about our questions. He is not offended or put off by our honesty. We all have questions. It would not be called faith if it was obvious or easily understandable. Following Jesus is referred to as walking by faith because there is always an unseen, can't-quite-comprehend-it element that requires us to be a little uncomfortable.

This is not because God delights in making us squirm. It's not because God enjoys watching us try to wrap our feeble minds around complex and mysterious concepts. It's simply because walking by faith is the essence of trust. It is not meant to be something we can fully understand and therefore control. The mystery of faith is not that it is hidden and hard to quantify. Faith is mysterious because it beckons us to come closer. It draws us in and peaks our curiosity.

God loves this. He loves to reveal Himself to us in layers. Faith keeps us on our toes – not in a way that causes us to constantly wonder if we are doing everything right, but in a way that causes us to lean in towards God. Faith keeps us curious about what God will do next and why. This is a particularly hard reality to adopt if we are dealing with hurt in our hearts.

Outwardly my life was pretty amazing. I had wanted to be a youth pastor for as long as I could remember and now my husband was a youth pastor. Close enough for me to check that off my list. We were serving at a great church that was growing really fast. Every pastor's dream! Check! I had always wanted to marry a strong Christian man and have kids. Check and Check. Financially, we were able to pay all of our bills and were living in a good house in a good neighborhood. Yet another check. There was little that could be seen as problematic.

Yet I was struggling. Really struggling. I could not even articulate what I was struggling about but the symptoms were there. I wanted my husband to love me in a way that felt more fulfilling. I wanted to feel important, loved, and valuable. I wanted to love my life but I was constantly finding a reason not to. I wanted to be someone else. I was always a little too intense about Jesus for my friends. I was too black and white about life. I could go on and on. There was so much tension under the surface.

In hindsight, I wish I would have gone to counseling much sooner. I wish I would have encouraged myself to put my fears on paper - to call out the things I was unknowingly believing about God that were endangering my emotional well-being. I wish I would have given myself permission to love who I am. At the time, I could not have done that because I truly did not know what God would say. That was the passive aggressive nature of my suspicions.

Maybe you can relate to my story. Maybe you have a hunch that God just doesn't like you as much as some of His other children. Maybe you wonder at times if He has given you all He has to give to you. Maybe you wonder if your lot in life is to be the one that toils in vain, working hard to obey His calling but never seeing any fruit. These suspicions are painful. We almost can't bear to ask God directly about them because what if He agrees with us?

At the time, I did not have the guts to actually ask the Lord if He wished I was someone else. I never asked Him if He wished I was skinnier, or if He thought I was close to what would make Him proud but not quite there yet. What would I do if my suspicions were correct? It felt better to not even ask in the first place.

I hope you know that all of those thoughts are lies. Every single one of them. God doesn't wish you were someone else or He would have made you someone else. It is as simple as that. He is trustworthy and He can handle your emotions. In fact, He invites them. Be honest with Him. Be raw. Be real. Don't hold back. And don't hang up the phone before He gets to talk. Unload on Him if you need to, but then quiet your heart and give Him a chance to speak to you.

Anger is often the outward behavior of an inward fear. It is a sign that we are protecting something internally, whether it is good or bad. God sees the fears hiding in our hearts. He would much rather speak to those fears than rebuke us for feeling angry. That's what a good Dad does. He sees what's fueling our emotions and hurt and He works to heal those places. Our job is to let Him.

Those years were the worst times of my life and yet, oddly, they became the best times. Something happened to me under the surface and between the lines of those stories. Something changed deep inside me that flipped the tables on everything the enemy was trying to accomplish through those dark moments. By the end of 2012 I understood something I desperately needed to understand all along... God's perspective.

I was searching and looking for someone, anyone, to help me get out of my pain. I looked to father figures, friends, family, and even my husband. I felt so empty trying to suck help from them because I was missing one key revelation. A simple insight I had been blind to all of my life. Jesus had already given me a way out and now I needed to give it to myself. How can we thrive when we're in the midst of such heartache and loss? The answer lies in our perspective and our connection with Jesus and His Holy Spirit.

Under the surface of these stories is a progression of a shifted perspective. As I did the hard work of uncovering all the wrong beliefs that were hidden in my heart, I entered a new level of freedom. As it turns out, rock bottom is only a vantage point and not a final destination. Everything we go through can be turned around. God can bring us into a life we never dreamed we could have. This isn't false hype. It is an honest testimony.

There is a peace waiting for you that will blow you away. There is a confidence available to you that will astonish you. There is a depth of love and acceptance for who you are that will exceed your every expectation. I know, it sounds too good to be true. But this is God we are talking about. Too good to be true is basically just another way to describe who He is!

There is one more thing you need to know. You have been given permission to thrive! You do not need anyone to tell you you're worth it. Jesus has already said you are. You can have a life of freedom, joy, and peace. You can have a life of fulfilling relationships and stability. I can't wait to show you how!

chapter two

THE BEST OF TIMES

One April morning in 2012 I was awakened suddenly by my husband. He had just returned home from staff pre-service prayer at our church. He informed me that he had volunteered us to host the guest conference speaker for lunch at our house. This particular guest speaker and prophet was a personal hero of mine. He had been speaking at our church conference the whole weekend and I had missed most of it because my third baby, who was only 2 months old at the time, was not having a good weekend.

I jumped out of bed in a panic and started to tidy up the house. We had three kids under five years old and "tidy" was not a battle I cared to fight often. My mind started racing. What would we talk about? Would he like us? Would he give me a prophetic word? My panic was palpable. I wanted to back out. I tried to get Grant to cancel. He assured me everything would be fine.

I mustered up the courage to think about what I would say at this lunch, and how I could make the most of this opportunity. If this man was willing to give me advice, what advice would I ask for? I managed to keep my cool as the lunch started. After some small talk and the chance to hear some of his amazing stories, I began to feel comfortable enough to let my guard down.

"Can I ask you an honest question?" I said. I mustered my courage, thinking that after all, I might never have a moment like this again in my life. What was there to lose? "Sure," he replied. I began to share a little about my frustration with my life, and how it was not panning out as I thought it would. Sure, there was a lot to be thankful for, but there was also an enormous pressure I could not find a way out from under.

I dove head first into sharing my story and then I simply said, "How do I get out of this?" He chuckled like a wise man hearing a question from a child. Then he joyfully replied, "You'll get out of it when you learn to love it." I sighed and accidentally blurted out, "So I guess I will never get out of it. How do you learn to love something that feels so terrible?"

NEW PERSPECTIVE

That day my life changed forever. It was not an instant change, but seeds were planted deep in my soul that grew into the harvest I now live and feed myself from. What unfolded in that moment was a transfer of wisdom from God. That wonderful man began to unpack the way of the kingdom for me.

"Rachel," he began, "You will learn to love the difficulty when you realize you are no more distant from God in the valley than you are on the mountain top. The love of God and the presence of God are constantly turned 100% towards you. Whether you are on the mountain top of life where you can feel that 100%, or whether you are in the lowest valley, God's presence is the same."

I listened attentively as he expounded on these truths. He continued to explain that we have the same access to God in the valley as we do on the top of the mountain. When this becomes our mindset we are no longer bothered by our circumstances. Circumstances are no longer able to affect our awareness of all that God is for us. Essentially what happens is that we gain a new perspective, and the valleys disappear. Instead of highs and lows there are now only different opportunities to experience God in a way that we could not experience or encounter Him when life is going well.

I sat there stunned at the words I was hearing. I had no concept of how to live from that perspective, but I knew that what I was hearing was truth. My only option, as I saw it, was to purpose myself to bring that perspective into my life as quickly as possible. That man gave me a key that day that I want to give to you. It's a simple question that can unlock the door of understanding.

> *Lord, who are you being for me, because I am in this situation, that you could not be for me if my life was where I wanted it to be?*

For me, the question began like this: "Jesus, who are you being for me in this moment, when I really do not like my life at all, that you could not be for me if I was really loving my life?" It sounds simple, but it is truly quite profound. In every circumstance there is an opportunity to see or experience something of God if we train ourselves to look for it. The worst of times can become the best of times if we realize God is right in the middle of it all revealing more of Himself to us.

God has made arrangements for you to have a great life with Him. The first step is to begin to look for Jesus and what He is doing in your life right now. Zero in on it. Call it out. Make it a big deal, because it is! You have not been abandoned or forsaken. You have not been left in a pit of your own misery. God is there with you. Put your focus on what God is doing right now in your life then dive in to what God has made available to you. Understanding what's available happens as you dig into the Bible and claim the promises of God for yourself. Let the Bible truly become a source of inspiration for you.

My perspective began to shift when I realized I was always connected to the presence of God. I realized I was the one choosing to withdraw or ignore what the Lord was doing in my life. It is an easy thing to do because we often know what we want God to be doing. However, what we want is not always what we need and God knows that. He is faithful to give us what we need so we can become someone who can steward what we want.

As I focused on what God was actually doing and let go of what I wanted or hoped He would do, I found a little niche of His presence that was carved out just for me. Once I identified that place, I was able to start looking for it when life got tough and things weren't going well. If I was feeling the sting of my pain and brokenness I would make the choice to stop standing in the pain shaking my finger in God's face. I would start looking around the landscape of the sorrow to find where God was shining His light.

There is no circumstance that the Lord doesn't work through. Sickness, tragedy, failure, broken trust, loneliness, and the like are all opportunities to find Him at work in our lives. Recognizing God at work in these moments does not mean dismissing the pain or being in denial of our difficulties. It merely means we make the choice to move towards God when all the circumstances are shouting at us to move away. Jesus is the best person to help us process what we are going through. Choosing to find Him in the tough times of our lives is one of the best things we can do.

For me, it took time. I had become so used to blaming God and taking my anger out on Him. I mistakenly thought He was annoyed that I was not more positive about my life. I assumed that He was frustrated that I was not focusing more on the blessings I did have instead of thinking about my difficulties. I had to remind myself to live differently until the perspectives and promises of the Bible became my new nature. As I began to use that key question, I found answers that startled me. I would write in my journal, "Jesus, who are you being for me today, because I don't know how to trust you, that you couldn't be for me if I wasn't so mad at you?"

I would put my pen on the paper and wait. He began to whisper things like, "I am building trust with you." Other days His answers would be, "I am your constant source of joy." "I am your comfort. I am your hope." I took those words to heart and thought about them constantly. What was unlocked within me was incredible. I owe a lot to that prophet for bringing me out of my darkness and into Jesus.

I call this tool "kingdom awareness" because God is always up to something and that something is always good. We are the ones who are not always aware of it. Kingdom awareness is the practice of paying attention to what God is actually doing in our lives right now.

It was this key that kept me connected to His presence as even greater sadness came into my life later that year as we said goodbye to our son. I consistently thank the Lord that I did not let those words fall flat after that lunch. I owned them as my own and I practiced them. That is what we have to do if we want to move forward.

Friend, I want to tell you something important…It's not enough to just scratch the surface of freedom in Jesus. We are not called to live barely free as if saved from our sins only by the skin of our teeth. We are called to live abundantly free.

I am a dreamer to the core. I love to dream, strategize,

brainstorm, and come up with great ideas. I love to learn and understand how to do different things. As a creative person, the idea is often the thrilling part for me. The act of making the idea a reality is not nearly as exciting. I always seem to struggle with implementation. But I have learned the hard way that dreaming and doing are two different skills. Dreams and strategies do not accomplish themselves. We have to implement our dreams if we want to actually achieve them.

I'm guessing you are reading this because you are serious about moving forward in your faith. I plan to continue to fill these pages with motivation. But I know that motivation is pointless if there are not concrete tools you can implement. I don't want you hoping you can get out of whatever is holding you back. I want you actually out of it! I want you thriving. So let's get practical!

BULLDOG FAITH

How do you take the truth of scripture and make it a reality in your life? Become like a bulldog. Honest confession moment: I am not an animal person. I would probably be completely satisfied in life to never touch another animal again. But even an animal-indifferent person such as myself knows that animals are God's creations too. There are qualities in animals that reflect the nature of God just like humans do. Take the bulldog for example. Bulldogs have extremely powerful jaws that can clamp down in such a way that it is very hard to get loose from their bite.

The bulldog shows us a vital principle in the kingdom of

God. Holy tenacity. If we want to get out of the frustration of our lives then we have to act like a bulldog. This is what we must do with the truths that we find in scripture. We must clamp down on those truths, bite really hard, and refuse to let them go until they become a part of us. We must never let go of the pursuit of God's presence and His promises of hope, joy and peace, even though it may take some time for those promises to actualize in our lives.

Back to that epic lunch meeting that changed me forever. The gut wrenching reality that I had to face was that my breakthrough would require me to dig deep and put a lot of practice into my faith. Of course, I didn't have to do that. I could stay in that place of yuck and stuck that I had become so acquainted with.

That is not what I wanted for my life. Somewhere, deep down, I knew it didn't have to be that way. Yet there I was headed down a path towards apathy if I didn't make a change. There was nothing to lose by using the key that was given to me. What could it hurt to take this prophet's advice and see if it could help me?

It was only a few months later when I received the surprise of a lifetime and I learned that I was pregnant with our fourth child. Then, only a few months into the pregnancy, as I previously shared with you, we were surprised again to learn that he had made his way to heaven. Heartbroken and confused I did the thing that I had been doing since that lunch. I started looking for Jesus. I didn't feel a need to blame Him or withdraw from His presence. I needed to find Him. I can honestly say that was not my normal response before that lunch.

I had been through disappointments before, although different from this experience. During difficult times in the past my tendency had always been to back up a little bit and re-evaluate what I thought about God. I would mull over whether He really was faithful because my circumstance was telling me He was not. Weeks would often go by while I pondered my relationship with the Lord before I would start to tip-toe back to Him.

This time was different and it was that key that made the difference. I had trained myself not to step back and ponder in suspicion but to lean in and ask directly. And that is exactly what I did. Nearly everyday I would get out my journal and ask my questions directly to Jesus.

My journal is filled with pages that start with words like: "Who are you being for me today because my arms are empty?" "What are you doing in my life right now? Open my eyes and let me see where you are at work." His answers carried me. They gave me a new perspective and He became the shepherd of my grieving process.

One such day I was sitting on the patio of Starbucks taking in the gorgeous fall weather. A few weeks had gone by after delivering my stillborn child. As I sat there I asked the question I was now so good at asking. "Lord, who are You being for me today because my arms are empty, that You could not be if I was still pregnant with my son?"

As I closed my eyes I was undone by the vision that came to me. Jesus walked up from the parking lot and sat across from me at my patio table. I saw Him lean in towards me and we began to talk. His presence radiated around me as He shared His great love towards me.

Jesus shared with me how much He loved my heaven baby. He had given us the name Kingston for him which means "Kings Town". It was a completely fitting name now that he would live out the entirety of his life in the King's town. Sitting there with Jesus He talked to me about how Kingston had a purpose in life and it was to be a catalyst in my life. He was sent to usher me into a new level of my life with God and he had accomplished that plan.

These insights astounded me. My son had fulfilled his purpose. Would I have ever known this if I had not taught myself how to lean in when everything inside of me was telling me to pull away? I don't think so.

Full disclosure: not all of the questions I had for the Lord were answered. Some were never answered. Some would be answered years later, even after I had forgotten I ever asked them. The point is simple. Jesus is the way through whatever you are going through. He is the only one who can truly understand the specifics of your life. Look for Him. Lean into what He is doing and let go, for a moment, of what you think He should be doing.

God answered my questions with such a profound amount of His presence and I began to heal. My understanding of God grew dramatically during that season. Outwardly it was a terrible time. There were so many doctors visits, hospital stays, and medical bills. Yet I would gladly go back and do it all over again. Not because I love to feel pain, but because I discovered God so wonderfully in the midst of it.

I finally started thriving because I tapped into what had been made available to me through Jesus. His constant presence and tangible love invaded my life as I made the conscious choice to welcome it in. In fact, the more I looked for Him, the more I found Him. It turns out that the words of the prophet at that lunch were fulfilled. I got out of it when I learned to love it.

chapter three

TANGIBLE EXPERIENCE

God is always providing for us. He is always depositing little revelations and insights into us. He gives us tools, keys, and understandings we will need for the future. There are provisions already placed within us to help us navigate what we are experiencing in our lives right now. It is important for us to become aware that this is how God works. He is such a good God!

I became aware of this reality around the time that I was getting good practice using the kingdom awareness key that I shared with you in the previous chapter. Around that same time I discovered this second key had already been subtly at work even though I had not recognized it yet. This second key is what I affectionately call "tangible experience." God wants to be tangible in our lives so that we are not limited to experiencing Him on an intellectual level only. We can experience Him in very practical and real ways.

A DIVINE SETUP

My personal discovery of this came in what I call my Psalm 18 season. In fact, you have already read a lot about that season of my life. A few weeks before my fourth pregnancy came to such an abrupt end I was spending time with the Lord. He led me to Psalm 18. I enjoyed reading it, although I could not see an immediate application to my life at that point. Then I felt the Lord instruct me that my Bible reading should only be Psalm 18 until He said otherwise.

It was an odd request, but I did it. Little did I know that I would live out the words of that Psalm over the next nine months. Psalm 18 is a short account of David finding the cords of death wrapping around him. He cries out to the Lord and his words go into the very ears of God. God rips the heavens open, hides inside a cloud, and comes to David's rescue.

As I read this chapter week after week different verses would jump out at me. Some were so encouraging. Others would hurt. Verse 19, for example, felt like it jumped out at me and slapped me in the face.

Remember I shared with you that I was facing the threat of cancer after my doctor had found a tumor on my thyroid? They discovered the tumor while I was pregnant.

Now that Kingston was gone, the doctors were focusing their attention on the tumor. I had been praying for my healing. My church was praying and fasting for me, and we were all begging God to come and take the tumor away. Then one morning I read these words:

> *"He brought me forth also into a large place; He was delivering me because He was pleased with me and delighted in me."*
> *(Psalm 18:19 AMP)*

In an instant I saw a correlation between my healing/ rescue and God's feelings about me. I quickly shut my bible and tossed it down on my bed. Hot tears welled up in my eyes as I came face to face with my reality. I did not know for certain if God delighted in me. Everything inside of me felt exposed. I could not honestly say that I believed that God delighted in me. Certainly not enough to rip open the heaven's, hide Himself in a cloud and come to my aid.

It was a gut-wrenching moment for me. As it turned out, it was a divine set up. What I could not understand is that God does delight in me…in all of us. We are His children and He would gladly rip the heavens open for any one of us. My healing was not hinged on whether I believed that, but that is what it felt like in that moment. God knew He was going to bring this revelation into my life. He knew it before I was even aware that I had a tumor or that my son would not live. He gave me Psalm 18 to hold on to and it was a divine set up all along.

In the months that followed that gut-wrenching moment I discovered the delight of God in my life. It was really messy but seriously incredible. I came into a greater understanding of my identity. It is not enough to know what the Bible says about us as God's children. Thriving means living it out.

My identity, at that point in my life, was basically borrowed insights and observations. I would see people I admired and I would try to imitate their relationships with God. That can be helpful in some cases, but in general it is incredibly limiting.

We need our own experiences with God. We each need our own moments when we are living out the words of scripture. We need our own stories of when we meet face to face with the tangible love and delight of God.

When we face hard circumstances we learn what we really believe. Facades fade when we are truly desperate. Only the truth stands when our beliefs are exposed, even if that truth is not what we want it to be. Our identity has to be formed around who God says we are on a very personal level. These truths need to be solidified deep within us where they actually shape our actions. I want to explore a few of the foundational beliefs regarding our identity that we find in the word of God.

If you are like me, you have probably heard the scriptures I am about to share with you. My prayer is that your eyes would be opened to fresh revelation as you read them. Pay close attention if you are someone who resonates with my journey or if you are realizing that you have a borrowed identity. Each of these portions of scripture are actually invitations for you. God wants to bring these words into a tangible experience in your life if you will let Him.

THE REAL POWER OF THE CROSS

The cross and Jesus' ensuing resurrection is my favorite moment in history. I love it because in one breath we were given salvation, freedom, deliverance, victory, and purpose. From that point forward we have been invited into a life better than we could ever imagine.

The moment Jesus took His final breath on the cross was the turning point in eternity. It was a combination of a complex, multifaceted moment in time that touched every area of our lives. The punishment for our sin was paid for once and for all. The door of reconciliation to our place as children of God was opened. From that point forward everything changed.

What Jesus accomplished on that cross was not only for us to be saved from hell, nor was it only so that we could go to heaven. Both of those are significant benefits, but they are not the totality. One of the most important truths of the cross is that it reinstated our place in the family of God. Through the cross Jesus provided a way for us to have the living God dwell within us, bringing us into ultimate victory over anything that comes against us.

The book of Ephesians details the after effects of the cross so beautifully. One of my favorite passages of scripture is found in Ephesians 1:7-13. I have capitalized a few of my favorite parts.

> *"Because of the sacrifice of the Messiah, His blood poured out on the altar of the cross, we are a free people. Free of the penalties and punishments chalked up by all our misdeeds. And not just barely free, either. ABUNDANTLY FREE! He thought of everything, provided for everything we could possibly need, letting us in on the plans He took such delight in making. He set it all out before us in Christ, a long-range plan in which everything would be brought together and summed up in Him, everything in deepest Heaven, and everything on planet earth. It's in Christ that we find out who we are and what we are living for. Long before we first heard of Christ and got our hopes up, He had His eye on us, HAD DESIGNS ON US FOR GLORIOUS LIVING, part of the overall purpose He is working out in everything and everyone." (Ephesians 1:7-13 MSG)*

Before you move on I want you to go back and read that passage again out loud. Yes, you read that right....out loud. Read it as if you were preaching to yourself. Pretend you are your favorite preacher and proclaim that passage just like they would if they were preaching it directly to you.

There is powerful depth in those words. Hope. Destiny. Intention. Perspective. Provision. Purpose. Sometimes we need to preach to ourselves so that we can rally some hope within our hearts. God has designed you to live gloriously. To thrive! He has actually prepared the way for you to live

GLORIOUSLY! That is the apostle Paul's way of saying that you are set up to thrive in your life with God. Not only does God want you to love your life, He has done everything on His end for you to live free. ABUNDANTLY FREE.

God delights in His abundant nature. It is a central part of who He is. His generosity is not because of anything we have done to deserve such a gift. It is just how He operates. He always goes above and beyond. Exceeding expectations is His thing.

Abundantly, according to its definition, includes: plentifully, extremely, and in large quantities. There's nothing small about that word. There is nothing lacking within that picture. Abundant freedom has already been given to us. It is our gift straight from God's heart.

The truth of this passage has not always felt like truth to me. In the thick of my darkness I had no clue how to make my life feel free. Abundant freedom wasn't even on my radar! I would read verses like Ephesians 1:7-13 and think how nice they sounded, but there was always a chasm standing between those words and my real life. It's like I read these words through a lens that made them feel more like a hopeful metaphor instead of a concrete, factual reality.

When we change our perspective, we change our lives. Do you want to see abundant freedom happen in your life? Great! Begin by believing it is truly possible. Don't give up until it actually happens. Change your vantage point from one of subtle separation to one of trust. Don't question whether God's words are too good to be true. Position your heart to declare, "If these words are in the Bible, Lord, then you must be willing to apply them to me."

Let's get even more practical. Take this verse for example.

> *"The thief comes only to destroy, but I have come that they may have life and have it more abundantly."*
> *(John 10:10 ESV)*

Cynicism might read this and either gloss over it, diminish it, or dismiss it. "Nice words Jesus, but I'm not buying it. Guess you ran out of that abundant life when you gave it to everyone else but me."

Hope reads those same words with an entirely different perspective: "Jesus, my life feels anything BUT abundant right now. But I know you have promised me an abundant life. I want to see where you are moving in me so I can focus on what you're doing."

Truthfully, a lot of Christians are good at reciting something like that prayer while simultaneously feeling a little twinge of frustration. Under the surface there is often a doubt that is lurking. Our words say one thing, but our hearts and minds are secretly unsure if Jesus ever fulfills these promises at all. This is something we need to recognize if it is happening to us. Being in denial of what we are really believing will not help us. It just might be trying to destroy us.

When we discover ourselves secretly doubting the promises of God we need to look more closely at our doubt.

Could there be a thought or disappointment that has not been addressed that is fueling our doubt? If we pretend that our doubt is not there we can end up holding ourselves back from true progress. It's ok if that is where we are but we need to own it.

Our prayer needs to become something like this: "Jesus, my life feels anything BUT abundant right now. And honestly, I don't think you are going to do anything about it. I want to hope but I need proof too. I want to have faith but I don't want to be disappointed. I am asking you to meet me right where I am and help me let go of these doubts. Help me learn to trust you."

That is a prayer that will take you places in your faith. It's honest and God loves it. The best thing we can do is allow ourselves to be truly honest about our doubts, but then lean in closer to Jesus and ask Him to lead us out of that place. Acknowledging the emotions we have about God and His promises is only one part of the process. We also need to know what to do with our emotions once we've recognized them.

If we allow ourselves to focus on what we feel instead of what Jesus actually said then we end up with a belief system that is a contradiction. Our emotions are helpful indicators but they are not meant to be the sole director of our lives. We have been given both emotion and logic, and they are meant to work together. You may have been told that they are mortal enemies but God designed your emotions and your logic to be best friends. Changing our perspective involves letting our logical side grab hold of the promises of

God and state them to our emotions like facts.

I love emotion. I am a tried and true feeler. My feelings are typically the first thing I notice about a situation and my gut feelings are often a source of great guidance for me. My emotions help me get hyped up from a good sermon. They give me all the chills and feels when someone is testifying to the goodness of God in their life. They even seem to borrow other people's confidence to feed to me when I am uncertain about something. Emotions are great. No, they are awesome. But they are also liars.

Emotions don't know how to hold God's promises. They sense doubt and exploit it. They can exaggerate, manipulate, and misdirect us. We have to learn to use both sides of our brain when it comes to Jesus. Logic loves facts. Logic thrives on concrete data and predictability. Logic has the power to help us stand firm in our faith regardless of how we are feeling about life. Our logic and our emotions are not at war with each other. They are designed to be perfect partners.

The words of Ephesians chapter one were not written for us so that we could momentarily feel better about ourselves only to later shrink back into our mental prisons of insecurities, doubt, and lack of actual depth of faith in God. We can actually live gloriously. We really can be released from that darkness and begin to soar with a freedom we've never dreamed of.

I am living proof of the truth of this passage from Ephesians. God has brought me into a place in my life where I do live gloriously and free from tremendous weights and baggage I acquired over the years. Once I was a captive prisoner to insecurity, doubt, rejection, and pain. I realize now that this glorious living promise was available to me all along. I just didn't know it. Then I didn't know how to get it.

THE FACTS OF LIFE

We all need to train ourselves to let our logical mind hold the promises of God as facts.

> Fact: God truly delights in you.
> Fact: Jesus has called you into abundant freedom.
> Fact: There is no power stronger than the love of God.

When we lock truths like these down as facts in our minds we rise to see them achieved. We must not bring our understanding of the word of God down to the level of our experience. We must choose to let our experiences rise to what the word of God says. We need to experience what the word says and not stop trying until we do.

We all know gravity is a thing. It's a concrete fact that what goes up will come down. Being momentarily weightless in an astronaut simulation does not undo the fact that gravity is real. What kind of nonsense would it be for an astronaut to try and debunk the law of gravity because he had an experience where it didn't apply? Isn't that what we try to do with the Bible?

Don't read the words of Ephesians or other books of

the Bible and dismiss them because your experience has not measured up to the fullness of those words. Challenge yourself to raise the level of your experience to what the Bible is saying.

This is what it takes to enter that realm of glorious living that God has provided you. There will be bad days as you pursue this promise, but that doesn't change the fact that it actually is available to you.

The enemy hopes that your bad days and difficult circumstances will be enough to get you to let go of God. He will try to twist your emotions until you feel like freedom is unattainable, not practical, and just a metaphor in a book written 2000 years ago. That's because he knows it IS attainable, practical, and a very real reality that can be yours if you want it!

chapter four

WRESTLE MANIA

Freedom is an abstract concept. It's hard to wrap your mind around it until you have experienced it for yourself. For me, the path to freedom often looks like an epic WWE wrestling match. Just when you think you're winning you are knocked over with a chair you didn't even know was in the ring.

There were so many wrestling matches in my "learning to love it" journey. "Me vs. Who God Says I Am." "Me vs. My Calling." "Me vs. My Flesh." Each time I found myself wrestling with my identity. Often it seemed that just when my mindset had changed, when I was finally beginning to believe God's truth about myself, my circumstances would try to prove me wrong.

Some days I would feel like Maria Von Trapp from the Sound of Music; I was twirling on a hill, perfectly capable of handling my life with the exact amount of poise and grace needed. Other days I was certain God had abandoned me to a pit of despair. I often didn't know what to believe. Should I trust the true reality I was living in, or the seemingly imaginary one I was reading about in the Bible? The struggle was real.

The New Testament is filled with the tangible reality of freedom in Jesus, and yet so few of us really live that way. In general, Christians have lost touch with the dynamic power that became available to us through the cross. When Jesus became the final payment for our sin He made a way out of our mess. He died for our salvation and our freedom, so that we can be free from the effects of sin in our lives. He showed the way for the new man inside us, the born again inner man or woman, to wake up and thrive.

When we enter into a relationship with Jesus through salvation we also enter into this realm of freedom. There really is a world all around us where freedom not only exists, but is handed out with relentless generosity. When we are saved we are united with Jesus. We literally get re-positioned in Him in such a deep and powerful way that nothing can separate us from Jesus. This truth is reiterated many times throughout the New Testament. In fact, nine different times in Ephesians 1 we see a theme that we are now located in Christ.

At salvation we are placed into Jesus and He is in us. At that moment we become positioned in the realm where all the spiritual blessings are. Ephesians 1:3 states so plainly:

> *"Blessed be the God of our Lord Jesus Christ, who has blessed us in Christ with every spiritual blessing in the heavenly places."*
> *(Ephesians 1:3 ESV)*

Those spiritual blessings are all the things we have been looking for. They are the peace, joy, love, acceptance, approval, value, mercy, power, provision and everything else our hearts long for.

How can this be true? Why are so many of us not automatically experiencing this? The problem lies in our blindness. We are simply not aware of what has been given to us. It is a human pattern that stretches throughout nearly the entire Old Testament.

God's presence would manifest in the midst of the Israelites as a pillar of fire and they would complain because they were not in Egypt. It was as if they considered slavery to a tyrant a better option than God's presence! God would manifest Himself in their midst as a cloud of smoke and lightning and simultaneously the Israelites were smelting gold to make a statute of a cow they could worship instead.

The Pharisees around Jesus had the same problem. They were literally standing face to face with Jesus, the Messiah they had spent their entire lives begging and hoping for, and yet they could not see that He was the Son of God. Much like them, many of us acknowledge Jesus as Lord but we are blind to the new life that has been opened to us.

AWARENESS IS ESSENTIAL

Availability and awareness are not the same thing. When a store is having a clearance sale and the thing you have wanted and couldn't afford gets marked down to 60% it becomes available to you. But you will miss the sale if you do not know it is happening. Awareness is essential. We need to know what freedoms God has made available for us to have.

The enemy is hard at work twisting and distorting the truth about what Jesus has already accomplished through the cross. The devil couldn't stop the cross. He couldn't stop that eternity shattering moment from happening. He has already been defeated, and his days are numbered. He can't win, so now he is reduced to making a last ditch effort to try to diminish the full spectrum of all that happened on the cross.

He tries to convince us that the cross is for us to get into heaven. The enemy wants us to believe that our problems are too big, too messy, and too complicated for the work of the cross. This is the nature of our struggle. Who are you going to believe? Your Savior? Or your enemy?

The cross dealt with the issue of our sin and brokenness completely. Once we are saved, we are forgiven. There are no more hoops to jump through. We have been forever reconciled to our Father in heaven. And yet, amazingly, that is only half of the story. Our salvation is also about our sanctification. It is about the life we are called to live from this day forward.

Jesus did not stay on the cross. He rose from the dead, defeated death and sin, and now He is seated in heaven next to the Father. As a result, we are now righteous and redeemed co-heirs with Christ! That is what Romans 8:17 makes clear:

> *"And if we are His children, then we are His heirs also: heirs of God and fellow heirs with Christ." (Romans 8:17 AMP)*

Some translations say "co-heirs" instead of "fellow heirs" but the implication is the same. We are called to the same things, the same inheritance, the same ministry as Jesus. Whoa! How can that be? Aren't we just sinners! Not anymore we aren't. When we accepted the gift of salvation God changed our status from sinner to fellow heir. Of course this does not mean we are in any way are equal to Jesus. He alone is the Son of God, but it does mean that Jesus has invited us into a freedom that is equal to His.

When God looks at us now, He sees us through the filter of Jesus. Jesus' filter makes us look really, really good! When God looks at us now, He sees us with a profound and deep love. Through Jesus, God now sees us as free, empowered, glorious, capable, and His.

To reject this new reality is to say something like, "What a nice thought Jesus, that you would allow me the privilege of being a fellow heir with you. But I must decline. I am in no way capable of something like that. After all, I am just a sinner saved by grace. Then again, you already know that. I think I will continue to look at you on the cross and thank you over and over again for my salvation. All I ever do is fall short of how you've asked me to live, so I know I don't really have a right to be a fellow heir alongside of you."

How absurd would it be to say that to God who just sacrificed His greatest prize for you? And yet we think these types of thoughts way too often. We need to wake up and recognize what is available to us! What Jesus has done for us to have a good life…an abundant life!

Yes, we are still people who are dealing with sin, doubt, disbelief, and pain. But don't get stuck on that one part of the story. The cross is vital to the story of God, but it isn't the end scene. The credits of the movie aren't rolling right after Jesus breathed His last because there is an entire Part two.

FULLY GOD

If we end the story of Jesus with the cross, we miss the entire second half of the show. Yes, Jesus dies on the cross. But after that He defeats Satan, overcomes the power of sin and death, emerges victoriously from the grave, and ascends into heaven. The "roll credits" moment of Jesus' story is the resurrected, victorious Son of God now sitting at the right hand of His father having completed His work. If you are only familiar with the Savior part of Jesus, always focusing on the cross moment of the story, then I want to introduce you to Resurrected Jesus. And let me tell you, you are going to LOVE Him!

There is a freedom that comes from the victorious Jesus

who defeated death and hell AND ascended into heaven. Resurrected Jesus is unstoppable. His presence in our lives is THE most powerful force on the earth. Let me take this a little deeper. On the cross, Jesus had not defeated sin and death yet. While He was on the cross His divinity was still embodied in a fully human form. Until He breathed His last, He was bound by the limitations of humanity. Once Jesus rose from the dead He entered into His natural and eternal state: fully God.

No longer is He limited in any way, shape, or form, and we must learn how to see Him in that light. It's the cross and the absolute intensity of His surrender that made the way for all of it. However, the cross was not the final destination. Jesus is capable, willing, ready, and eager to break your chains. We need to learn to expect Him to show up in our lives in this way.

Focusing too much on the picture of Jesus on the cross has a way of subtly keeping us looking at ourselves through a lens of defeat. We laser focus on what we are lacking, what we can't get together, how we can't measure up, and so on. Although that is the appropriate way to approach Jesus at the point of our salvation, we are meant to move beyond that perspective. To stay there, in that posture and viewpoint, is to stay at the front door of our house refusing to go all the way inside. When we choose to look at Jesus the Victor, the Accomplished, the Triumphant, the All Powerful, we have to look up to heaven to see Him.

When we are looking up we are no longer looking at ourselves and our limitations. We are seeing Him and where

He is at work in our lives. That is what the cross does for us! Life is no longer about us, how we struggle, the ways we fall short.

Now that Jesus is entirely fully God, life is about Him and His kingdom. That's why He instructed us to pray "Your will be done" in Matthew 6:10. It is not about our will and wants coming to pass. Our will is found in His will coming to fruition in our lives. This is a powerful key in beating the struggle. Jesus is at work in your life. You may not see it yet, but He is there.

We must fix our eyes on Jesus and what He is doing. When we find we're looking too much at ourselves, we need to just stop and refocus on God. Ephesians 1 is clear that God, our Father, has already taken care of every single thing we need to have an amazing life of freedom and abundance in our relationship with Him.

WRESTLING WELL

Who are the characters in your wrestling match? Have you identified them yet? The nature of our wrestling and struggle is the fight to decide what we really believe and how we will see those beliefs take shape in our lives. This was my struggle. I wanted to believe. At times I truly did believe. But I would inevitably get knocked down by moments where my life would not line up with those beliefs.

I found myself asking, "Do you really love me Lord? Why do I seem to always have a hard life and other people have it so easy? Why is it that no one really understands me? Are you going to let me see the purpose of my life? Will I ever be able to accomplish it if you don't tell me what it is?" And so on.

What we do when we are picking ourselves up off the floor is important. Do we acknowledge we are still in the waiting phase of seeing God become a promise keeper? Do we throw in the towel altogether? Do we pretend we never hit the ground at all?

Faith is so messy. I find it strange that no one really acknowledges that. Maybe it's because people don't want to be seen as having questions. Are we afraid that our questions will cause other people to question? Maybe. But I find strength for my journey when I hear my leaders share about their wrestling matches. Every leader has them. Every human has them. We were never asked to not question Jesus. We were never instructed to blindly accept every single thing we hear or see from God. We were only ever asked to trust and follow Him.

The questions you are asking are important to the Lord. Do you want to know how you can tell what area of your life God is getting ready to work in next? It's the area of your biggest questions. The one that gives you pain right now. You know that thing that you are so hoping God will do for you? You want it so badly you find stinging tears welling up in your eyes when you talk about it.

I am not suggesting God is going to do exactly what you are hoping for. But I am saying He wants to wrestle through that part of your life with you. He wants to speak into that area of your heart. Your tears are the proof that He is already preparing you for that encounter with Him.

We have to engage in the wrestle mania. We can't play dead when these thoughts come at us in full force. We can't pretend we know the answers. We can't dismiss the struggle in fear that it won't end well. We have to fight. We need to put our spandex on, get in the ring, and go after the Lord with our questions. We need to believe we are strong enough to struggle well. Let me tell you a secret...Jesus is strong enough to handle us while we do.

The Bible is literally full of great wrestlers. Abraham and Sarah wrestled for twenty-five years from the point where they were first called to the moment they had Isaac. Jacob quite literally and physically wrestled with God. Moses wrestled. David wrestled. Hezekiah wrestled. Pretty much everyone in the Bible that we admire had a season where they wrestled with what they knew about God and how to follow Him. Even Jesus wrestled with God before He went to the cross.

We must not shy away from the questions we are having. We need to take them straight to the Lord in conversation and take them to trusted mentors in our lives. We need to name them, acknowledge them, and say what they are. We must take the time to think about what we are struggling with. What is the exact nature of it? Once we understand that we can talk it out. That recognition sets us up to wrestle and win.

What does winning look like? Growth. Resolve. Insight. A good struggle with the Lord is one where we don't tap out early and miss the blessing that comes at the end. Instead, we stay engaged with the Lord as long as it takes to get to the point where we truly understand and get a breakthrough.

God has already given you a tool to help with this. It's a secret weapon of sorts and it is in you right now. We will explore that incredible secret sauce in the next chapter.

chapter five

YOUR SECRET WEAPON

Are you ready to learn about that incredible gift that is hiding within you right now? Your God-given, often unnoticed secret weapon? I truly believe this is one of those moments of sheer mastery and brilliance on God's part. You were given a brain. In fact, medically speaking, you cannot be considered alive without one. Your brain is your hidden superpower, your secret weapon, and the key to your breakthrough.

However, let's not forget that your brain is an organ. Just like your heart, stomach, liver and other organs, your brain is designed to work in a specific way. Think about it like a line of computer code or an algorithm. Coded into your body's organs are natural functions that happen without your involvement. Your organs are working for you.

For example, you are breathing right now because the code in your lungs is doing what it was designed to do by inhaling oxygen and exhaling carbon dioxide. Your stomach works for you by digesting your food according to its God-given process. Your heart works for you by circulating your blood through your body, and so on.

Unlike our other organs, however, the brain is where we think so we often confuse the biology of the brain with who we are. We, as humans, are spiritual beings. We are not merely mammals or the product of some evolutionary accident. We are spiritual beings designed in the image of God. You would never proclaim, "I am my liver and my liver is me!" Right?!? Yes, you need your liver but you also inherently understand it is a part of your body as a whole.

You are not your brain. Just like your other organs, your brain works for you. Your brain is following its natural coded design by processing your thoughts, among other things. That processor is amazing and it is designed by God to help you move forward in your life. So how exactly is that a spiritual tool? Let's take a closer look at what is happening in your brain right now.

The brain works like a catalog system. It is designed to take a new thought, automatically search all the previously stored thoughts you have, and then catalog that new thought accordingly. It is automatically comparing these words you are reading right now to things that you have heard that are similar and opposite. You may have noticed moments of recall happening where memories are quickly popping up of moments these words remind you of. That is your beautiful brain at work.

Can you see how your brain is one of God's most incredible gifts to you? It is designed to help you live a powerful life. It's also the primary battle ground of your struggle. Your brain is not your enemy. You need to understand what the brain has been designed to do and use that to your advantage.

I love the brain. Maybe I am secretly a mega-nerd at heart, but the brain fascinates me. I don't consider myself an expert, however, more like a brain hobbyist. My hope in these pages is to somehow translate brain science into modern day terms to try and illustrate how amazing your brain is. I am not trying to school you at a college level. I am simply giving you an overview of how your brain works on a very practical level. If you can wrap your mind around this you will be unstoppable.

Science has proven that you live the bulk of your life from a subconscious state of mind. The routines you have, the way you think and respond, and how you process life happens from the subconscious part of your brain. In other words, it is happening on autopilot.

You wake up and go about your morning routine because you have been doing the same thing every day. You gravitate towards the same types of foods and time to eat your meals because at some point you ate them regularly enough that it became your habit. How do these daily habits make it to the subconscious? At some point in your past, there were deliberate choices in the conscious part of your brain that were repeated often enough that they were then passed on to the subconscious part of your brain. Now those actions run your life.

The same is true for your thoughts. Think something long enough and it will become second nature for you. The term "second nature" is just another way of recognizing the subconscious at work. You have been doing something so regularly you don't even have to consciously think about it anymore.

How is your thought life? Are negative thoughts a daily thing for you? What thoughts do you have repeatedly? For example: does your reflection in the mirror trigger a barage of negative thoughts? Congratulations. You have just discovered your subconscious at work in your thought life.

It is a sobering realization but there is hope. The good news is that your brain is also designed to change and adapt. You can change the thoughts that are running your auto-pilot and sitting in your subconscious right now. It's called neuroplasticity.

This concept may seem far-fetched and unlikely for a book about following Jesus. But here is the God's honest truth…God made your brain. Brain science is simply unveiling the brilliance of our Creator. This is one of those moments where the scientific world meets the spiritual world and the result is a cataclysmic revelation that absolutely will make your life better.

YOU ARE NOW A NEW CREATION

Before we continue with our science lesson we need to

look at how salvation throws a kink in the brain's operating system. This is because we were not created to live apart from relationship with God. When you were saved you became a new person. There was a spiritual re-birth that occurred that was every bit as powerful as your first birth into the world.

Your born-again moment did two things. First, it brought forth a newly redeemed creation that is now united and joined with Jesus. (Think of your best self and then super-charge it!)

Second, it separated this new self from your old self. The old self is the sinful nature. This old self, in God's eyes, is not redeemable. It is not needed for your new life in Christ. Your old self is what Romans, Ephesians, Colossians, Galatians, 1 Peter and other books of the Bible refer to when they describe the part of you that was not born again at your salvation.

Consider a butterfly that has just emerged from a cocoon. This new creation began its life as a mere caterpillar that went through an epic transformation resulting in an entirely new creation. It now has an entirely different DNA makeup. And yet, that new butterfly creation was hiding within the caterpillar all along. Even the ingredients for the cocoon, the place of transformation, were hiding inside the caterpillar. When the butterfly emerged it left behind both the caterpillar residue and the cocoon.

Both the residue of the caterpillar and the cocoon are left with a part of that butterfly in them, but both are now obsolete to the life of the new, beautiful butterfly. This is one of the most amazing natural parallels to salvation. You are now a new creation. The old you is gone, obsolete and unnecessary for where you are going in life - so much so that God calls the old self dead. It is not coming back. You don't need it anymore.

Here is where it gets interesting. Your old self is stored in your memory and in your subconscious. The patterns of your old self, the temptations and the beliefs, are stored there as well. A huge part of your struggle is the wrestling between what you always thought and believed in your old nature, verses what you now believe as a new creation. This is precisely why Romans 12:2 commands us to renew our minds.

We have to tell those old patterns that they are old news. In doing so, we are storing new thoughts into our subconscious. Why do we need to do this? So that we can live from the place of the new creation God has brought forth in us.

You are now a new creation. There are new ways of thinking and new autopilot patterns that God wants to put into you. Your job is the process of confronting the old thoughts and replacing them with God-thoughts. Your brain was designed by God to work this way, and this process will help you move forward once the old patterns are gone. This work is the part you play in your transformation. It is the practicing of our faith. God has given you the tools and now it's up to you to implement them.

Look at it like building a foundation. Your subconscious is the foundation of your life. You want it to be healthy, strong, and secure. You want to be able to read scripture and accept it. You want to be able to receive a promise of something good God wants to bring into your life, and not reject or doubt it. You want to have the courage to stand on truth when you are in a hard season.

All of these things happen when you have a good foundation in your subconscious. Renewing your mind is the process of replacing the unhelpful and unhealthy thoughts in your subconscious with thoughts that are in line with the Bible and who God says you are. The end goal is for your "auto-pilot" thoughts and actions to help you as you journey with Jesus.

I could fill another book with my own stories of this process. I have replaced so many thoughts and actions over the years that I can hardly remember them all. But I will never forget the moment Holy Spirit pointed out how many times I thought, felt, and said that I was overwhelmed.

The truth is, my life is a little hectic these days. With four young kids, a church to pastor, and running four businesses there is never enough time to get everything done. Over time I started to think and admit that I was overwhelmed. I would agree with people who told me I was busy and had my hands full. Is that really wrong? It depends. It was wrong for me because God had called my family to each of these things and He had supplied ample amounts of grace to manage it all.

Every time I bought into the idea of being overwhelmed I was rejecting the sufficient grace God was supplying. The truth is that we manage our lives well. We take days off, are intentional and present at home, and spend ample amounts of time with Jesus. So, in fact, I wasn't overwhelmed. The more I would tell myself I was overwhelmed the more I would feel stressed. I found that I was less motivated to fulfill my calling and more interested in binge watching a show because I felt I deserved some down time.

When Holy Spirit nudged me that day He spoke conviction into my heart. He challenged me to press into the grace of God and reject the lie. So I did. When I would catch myself admitting to someone that I was overwhelmed I would literally stop and say something like, "Well, I guess it's not that overwhelming. I am experiencing the grace of God and God is taking care of us."

Every time I noticed I was thinking about feeling overwhelmed I would stop myself and pray, "Lord, this life you have called me to is truly a gift. Yes, we are running fast and hard but I will let you have your way in my life. I receive your sufficient grace you've given for today."

It took about two weeks before I noticed something changing. The thought was coming less and less. And when it did come it came with a desire to pray as well. Weeks later I did not resonate with the idea of being overwhelmed at all and I was ready for God to add yet another thing to my plate!

If you do not actively renew your mind you will keep struggling. Those old self thoughts will continue to come back to the forefront of your mind until you tell them what to do. So often we struggle as we try to figure out why we are doubting God, or drawn to sin, or afraid of God, etc. To change our patterns we need to do the hard work of replacing our old thoughts and the residue of our old nature that is waiting to be confronted and changed.

EMPOWER YOUR BRAIN

How exactly does this happen? The more you think about something the more it becomes a part of you. Your brain is malleable and it adapts to what you are most focused on over time. Your brain builds literal, physical matter called neural pathways around the thoughts you focus on the most.

For example, when you spend years of your life looking at yourself in the mirror and hating what you see, you have actually created fortified, strong physical highways of thoughts inside your brain. This is why, for example, it's so hard to believe it when people tell you how beautiful you are. According to your brain you have loads of evidence that says otherwise.

Have you have spent years of your life believing you have to earn God's love through giving money, time, or serving? Then those thoughts have become physical matter in your brain. They are fortified patterns that won't be undone in a day. When you start to change this, your brain starts speaking up. When the catalog coding can't find supporting evidence of your new revelation it starts trying to flush out and forget these new thoughts. This is the way your brain is designed to work.

Essentially what is happening is that your brain is running a program to keep you going in the direction you are already headed. Your brain doesn't know if you like that direction or not. It doesn't really care if it's a healthy way to think or behave. It just knows your patterns have conditioned your brain to think this way. This is what it has been hard-wired to do. Your brain knows your patterns and when something contradicts those patterns it will get tucked away and placed out of sight until proven to be more than a fleeting thought.

If you want to change the thoughts that are running your autopilot you have to have new thoughts. You need a lot of new thoughts. The best thing you can do is to declare truth over yourself. Take time everyday to have focused thoughts about the goodness of God, the reality of His love for you, the incredible gift of His mercy, and so on.

Read the Bible, memorize scripture, and pray out loud. Talk to your friends about what God is teaching you and speaking to you. As you do this your brain catches on that there is a new you emerging. It will start building strong, fortified highways of thought that compel you towards God and His word.

But what happens when you do all of that and then some old thoughts start creeping back in? Let's refer back to the coding your brain is operating on. There is a limited amount of storage space in your brain. As time goes on, your brain runs something like a self-clean application that goes through the catalog of your thoughts and experiences. When it's been a while since you have truly thought about something, your subconscious will send that thought to the forefront of your mind to give you a chance to see what you think about it.

That is your opportunity to take that thought captive and replace it with a new thought. If you are convinced you do not believe that thought anymore it actually goes away and gets replaced by what you think now. If you do want to think that way, then that thought goes happily back to where it came from and keeps silently running the show.

Have you ever stopped to consider that maybe it is your old self's thought residue that creeps up when you are struggling or feeling tempted? Your thoughts don't care if you want to keep them or not. Remember, you absolutely have the power to change them.

This process of old thoughts re-surfacing is the coded program they are running on. It's their job. It is how they sort and process information. This is where your brain becomes your secret weapon. You get to determine if you want your thoughts to line up with Jesus and the Bible or not. Your spirit, that eternal part of you, is actually calling the shots here...not your brain.

BODY, SOUL, AND SPIRIT

Most of us accept the truth that we have a spirit that is eternal. What we need to understand is that there are three parts of us that are designed to work in perfect harmony together. We are not only an eternal spirit. We have a soul and we have a body. Our spirit is the part that is united with Jesus. Our body, the flesh and human part of us, is the form we take on this earth. Our soul is the partially supernatural and partially natural part of us. It is like the glue that connects our spirit to our body.

Your soul is designed to follow the lead of your spirit, which is designed to follow Jesus now that it is united with Him. Your soul then translates that into your body and your brain. This is how life is supposed to go for you. You are designed to be led by Jesus, following His lead with joy and peace. Your body, brain, thoughts, emotions, and actions are designed to follow His lead also. However, it is possible to be saved and yet not live in this way.

I want you to realize something…you are victorious. You are capable of rising above your old patterns and temptations. Jesus is with you. All the thoughts that tell you otherwise are thoughts that are not submitted to the Lordship of Jesus. There's a chance that you are experiencing this right now. When we let anything but Jesus and His truth run our lives things get whacky. Don't worry, it is completely fixable.

The daily process of changing our thought patterns can be a struggle. I know this first hand. Transformation, and I mean lasting transformation, does not happen overnight. It happens day by day as we focus our thoughts on Jesus, His kingdom, on God and our identity as His children. It is the consistency of our thoughts that makes the biggest difference.

What about those of us who grew up knowing Jesus and were saved from an early age? This process applies to us as well and the process of renewing our minds is the same. Struggles are rooted in a version of ourselves that is not the fullness of what God has for us. We are on a constant path of becoming more like Jesus. Every time we grow into a new way of thinking and living for Jesus, we will have to retrain our minds. Thankfully, the process gets easier and more smooth the more we go through it.

Here is one more crucial action point for your action plan. Remember how I told you that right before those old-self thoughts really go away for good they come back to the forefront of your mind to check in and see if you still want them? This part of the process is a bit like that ex-boyfriend that just won't get out of the picture.

After you have repeatedly scorned his advances he makes one final, ill-timed, grand gesture to win you back before he really moves on. These old thoughts are like that. When they come up to the forefront of your mind they can be so convincing. They often feel so strong. They will stand there as if in imaginary rain, making puppy dog eyes while hoisting a boom box over their head.

Scientifically, the last attempt the old thoughts make before they go away for good is the strongest one of all. It will feel like everything in you wants to compromise. Stand strong in that moment. Don't give in. Just don't. Do not let yourself feel defeated if you still have an old thought creeping back up.

It doesn't mean that you are not powerful or that you are not experiencing victory. It means those thoughts want to see if you really mean no. It's nothing personal to the thought itself. It is just doing what it was programmed to do, which is to keep you thinking what you want to keep thinking. Don't get off track when it comes up to check and see one more time if it really is a real no. Just stand firm!

chapter six

SPIRITUAL WARFARE

There is something I need you to know. You have an enemy. Gosh I hope you already know that. I couldn't risk writing this entire book and not mentioning one of the big factors that might be at work in your life. Spiritual warfare is real. You are a threat to the demonic realm. The devil so wants you dead, dis-empowered, broken-down and deceived. That is his plan and he is hard at work at it.

Ephesians 6:16 tells us that he often works this plan by shooting fiery darts at us. These fiery darts are like thoughts that come out of no where aimed to bring us down. Second Corinthians 10:5 tells us to take these fiery dart thoughts captive and get rid of them.

Another way the enemy works his plan is by orchestrating the circumstances around us to manipulate us into coming into agreement with him. This is the oldest trick in the book. It is exactly what he did with Eve in the garden of Eden, it's what he did to Jesus in the wilderness, and it's what he will do to you when he gets the chance.

Our agreement is powerful. It is how we empower the different areas of our lives. The enemy knows this and will work to get you to agree with his thoughts and plans in any way that he can.

How can you overcome the enemy's plans to harm and hinder you? The answer is to just say no. Say no to the agreement. Say no to the invitation to believe the lie. Say no to the enemy's plan for your life. I think this probably feels overly simplistic, but your "no" is so much more powerful than you think.

Grasping this reality requires us to once again look at what happens through salvation. Once you are saved you are eternally united with Jesus. His power begins to work within you. He is on your side and actively working to bring about His will in your life and through your life. Let's examine our enemy for a moment.

There is nothing redeemable about satan. You may not have realized it, but the demonic forces that hate you are ultimately hating Jesus in you. They hate that Father God loves you unconditionally. They hate that Father God sees you as a precious, royal born and beloved child.

These forces of darkness can never have what you have now...access to the pure presence of God. Their fate is sealed. They've been cast out and they are not welcome in the family of God ever again. Because of that, they want to make you suffer. This battle between good and evil is a story that is being repeated in an endless cycle until Jesus comes back.

Think about it like this: What's the most common theme in action movies? In movie after movie the hero's greatest fear comes true. A loved one is captured, the bad guys make demands, and a ransom is sent. In the process the hero ignores wise counsel and gives up all common sense. Out of love, the hero runs straight into the chaos to rescue their most precious family member. I think this is a story we all love because it is THE story of our lives.

Father God's kids were tricked and taken captive by the enemy. God stopped at nothing to win them back. He even sacrificed the thing He loved the most, Jesus, to pay the ransom. God gets His kids back and yet the bad guy is still trying to kidnap them again. This is our daily struggle. The enemy wants to break God's heart by hurting us. But we have a say in the story of our lives!

We are no longer helpless little children who are easily lured into a stranger's van by a piece of candy. We are the kids who have been equipped with tools and gadgets to cut through the handcuffs, signal the rescue squad, and get back into safety.

As if that isn't enough, like an epic heist movie (think Ocean's Eleven), there has always been an entirely hidden sub-narrative at work. God comes out of this story of sacrifice more than the victor. Every scene demonstrates His masterful ability to turn even the worst moments around for good.

Make no mistake, God is working in your life. He is right in the midst of whatever spiritual battle you are facing right now. But He expects you to do your part, to remember your training and to access the provision He has placed inside of you. It's your job to partner with Him and His plan for your life.

Just say no to the schemes of the enemy! When you realize the devil is twisting truth, call it out! When you find yourself dodging fiery darts of self-doubt, insecurity, defeat, hopelessness, and fear, stop and take them captive! You'll be able to get rid of them because now you'll realize what is happening: The bad guy is using you as bait for the hero.

You are not a helpless victim. You are not someone God feels indifferent about. Those are some of the lies the enemy uses to manipulate you into ignoring the fact that the power of Jesus is sitting inside of you right now at this very moment.

Once you become aware of that power at work in you, the enemy will often try harder to convince you that you are wrong about God. He will start sifting through the catalog of memories and beliefs in your brain. He will manipulate and twist and distort. That is when your logic becomes a powerful tool. Stand on the facts of who God says you are and do not give up or give in until Jesus comes through for you. Just tell the enemy "No! I'm not signing off on your schemes and delusions anymore."

The enemy feeds off the power you give him. He has been

stripped of all the authority he once had. The only power he has left to gain over you is the power he gets from you.

Think about it. He is a helpless loser. In every sense of the word, he lost. I am not trying to minimize the strength of the attacks that have come against you. I am trying to show you how much more powerful Jesus is inside of you. You are really powerful too. Together with Jesus there is literally nothing you cannot overcome!

There was a time in my life when I would not have believed these words. I was twenty-one years old and newly married. Unbeknownst to me, I was about to discover one of my strongest spiritual gifts. My entire life I had a fascination with paranormal and dark things. Not like Wednesday from the Addams family but I really enjoyed day dreaming about supernatural things. As a child of a Southern Baptist mom and a Jewish dad I was not raised with knowing that God was supernatural. I guess I thought power was held almost exclusively by the underworld.

I loved reading stories about witchcraft, dragons, and other mythical tales. Something in me wanted to know there was a world in which supernatural things could be real. After I got saved I put aside those stories but the intrigue never died down.

As it turns out, I have the gift of discernment. It is an amazing gift that is rarely talked about these days because, well, it's weird. 1 Corinthians 12 listed it as the gift of discerning between spirits. Basically it is the ability to know whether something is from God, our flesh (or selfishly motivated), or the devil.

I did not know this was a thing until I was twenty-one. I began to have a series of night terrors that would result in paranormal activity in my mind and my house. To say I was terrified is a massive understatement. I could not figure out how to make this attack leave me alone.

Truth be told, I did not even understand it was an "attack." This went on for three months primarily in my mind. I would see demonic, horrifying, and dark images in my mind for hours as I would try to go to sleep. My typical bed time prayers were no match for what was happening.

Eventually the night terrors stopped but I was left with the undeniable sense that the enemy was way more powerful than I thought possible. I see now that the demonic realm was striking first because they knew I would be striking back. If they could get me to have a base-line of fear then I would proceed in following the Lord with caution. I would hesitate before I went after the enemy. I would think twice before engaging in spiritual warfare.

Over the years I came to a realization I wish I had in those days. Yes, the enemy is powerful. But he is no match for our God. Our God is THE God. He created all things on heaven and on earth! There is no competition. When satan was cast of heaven it was not a long and epic battle. It was no contest. God declared him gone and he was.

Somewhere along the lines I bought into the story that there was this huge battle of good and evil in the heavens. Maybe it was my brief understanding of Greek mythology mixed with my overactive imagination that had me thinking the battle was nearly lost by God. HA! The truth is I had bad theology and that bad theology bred a lot of fear into me.

THE WIN-WIN KINGDOM

The kingdom of God is a win-win kingdom. Even when we lose in life we win because we gain revelation, insight, compassion, etc. When we are in Christ we are on the winning side. Jesus empowers us to have no fear of the enemy or the demonic realm. This is the reality we all must renew our minds to.

Meditate on how big God is. Fix your eyes on the miracles Jesus worked in the gospels. Encourage yourself with the supernatural things God is doing on the earth today. Do not allow yourself to believe the enemy is more powerful than your agreement with Jesus. In Christ you have the upper hand. In Christ you have the key to breakthrough. In Christ you have access to everything you need.

When we say no to the devil we say no with the weight of King Jesus behind our words. When we say no to the strongholds in our lives we reverberate with the sound of heaven in agreement with us. When we say no to the enemy we take back the control in our lives so that we can then give it to Jesus. It is time to relinquish our fear of the enemy once and for all. He is no match for Christ in you.

Spiritual warfare is not just night terrors and paranormal stuff. It is the effort the enemy exerts to try and stop you. It is the obstacles that are thrown at you to weigh you down. Things like illnesses, chronic conditions, emotional issues, and relational breakdowns that seem to come out of nowhere. You can experience spiritual warfare in your finances, your personal property, and your career. Simply put, the enemy will try everything he can to stop you from moving forward with God.

Why do we have to deal with this? Can't we just snap our fingers and be done with the devil? Not exactly. The enemy and the entire demonic realm are on borrowed time. God will deal with them severely when the end comes. So why does he let them stick around? Is God afraid of the enemy? No, but He does have a few tricks up His sleeve.

Remember that God has an appointed time when Jesus will come back and the demonic realm will be no more. While we may not understand it we have to trust that He knows what He is doing.

What is He doing? He is preparing His body of believers to be like Him. Remember how we are made in God's image? One of the ways we are being made into His image is that we are being made into victorious warriors. We are being made into winners. We are being transformed into His likeness and He is not afraid of anything! That means we can live our life with confidence. We can take authority over what the enemy is trying to do and send him on his way.

I am guessing you have experienced spiritual warfare in your life. I suspect you will experience more in the future. So you need to know that the goal is not to be untouchable. The goal is that when we discover the enemy at work in our lives we know what to do. We know how to overcome. We know how to strike back. We know how to call on God and receive our breakthrough.

You will not be exempt from spiritual warfare. People experience different levels of it depending on your God-given calling, but no one is exempt. We all need to know how to fight. We all need to know how to defend ourselves. We all need to not be surprised when we see the enemy working in our lives.

There are a few ways to know you are encountering spiritual warfare.

1. No matter what you do you can't get free. Like a chain around your leg you keep getting yanked back to the same place in life.
2. Your circumstance is leading you away from a deeper relationship with Jesus.
3. Obstacles keep standing in your way of obeying the Lord.

Don't be discouraged if you find yourself dealing with spiritual warfare. In fact, you should be encouraged! The demonic realm has a limited amount of resources. God, as the creator of all things, has the ability to continually create whatever He wants to. The enemy is not like that. He has to conserve his resources so he doesn't waste his time. If you are encountering warfare then there is something significant going on in your life.

GOD'S ULTERIOR MOTIVE

There is one more uniquely bizarre aspect of warfare I want to share with you and it comes from Judges chapter three. In these verses we see something about the nature of God as a warrior and His intent to make us like Him. Take a look at the creativity and commitment God had in making His people more like Him.

> *"Now these are the nations that the Lord left, to test Israel by them, that is, all in Israel who had not experienced all the wars in Canaan. It was only in order that the generations of the people of Israel might know war, to teach war to those who had not known it before. These are the nations: the five lords of the Philistines and all the Canaanites and the Sidonians and the Hivites who lived on Mount Lebanon, from Mount Baal-hermon as far as Lebo-hamath."*
> *(Judges 3:1-3 ESV)*

What this is telling us is that God purposely left Israel surrounded by enemies. An entire generation had grown up not experiencing battle and God couldn't have that. He was focused on training them. The training would come from facing their enemy so God made sure they had plenty of enemies to choose from. He wasn't worried about their destruction because He was confident in His abilities to teach them how to be warriors. You know, God is really convinced that He is God and that He is the most powerful force there is!

It is important to the Lord that His people, those who bear His image, know how to be victorious even in the face of the enemy. No one is exempt. Why does this matter to God? Because this is God's reality. He is always victorious in the face of the enemy constantly coming up with different ways to wage war on your life. You are being transformed into a warrior. There might be battle on every side of you right now but that's ok. God is right there with you in the middle of it all!

If you are reading this and realizing you are in the midst of a spiritual battle I want to give you a key to help you. Begin to ask the Lord how He is training you through this battle. Ok, you caught me. This is the kingdom awareness key I told you about in chapter two. If you can begin to see how God is training you to be a warrior through this warfare then you will unlock a new level of perseverance and joy in the midst of your circumstances.

Here is one more little gift for you. This is my favorite, trusted, go-to prayer. It won't solve every spiritual crisis but it will help. This prayer is from Matthew 18:18 where Jesus tells us that we have the authority to bind up the work of the enemy and release the work of heaven. Essentially this prayer is a simple way to say no to the work of the enemy and yes to what God is wanting to do. It goes something like this:

> *"In the name of Jesus, I bind up every work of the enemy in my life. I bind up fear in Jesus name. (If you know the specific spirit that is behind the attack you can insert that here.) You cannot work in my life any longer. You must release your hands*

off of me. I bind up every scheme of the enemy and I declare that no weapon formed against me will prosper (from Isaiah 54:17). I loose the will of God over my life. I loose and release the atmosphere of heaven over my mind, my body, and my household. Cover me in your protection, Lord Jesus. Amen."

It might seem simple but there is power in that prayer. I often find myself praying it and marveling at how effective that simple act of binding up the bad and loosing the good truly is. Jesus meant it when He said those words in Matthew. However, not every difficult thing we face in life is caused by spiritual warfare. In the next chapter we will explore how to know if you are really experiencing an attack from the enemy or something else entirely.

chapter seven

WHERE DID THAT COME FROM?

I am a doctor's kid so my childhood was a little different than most. Having a dad who was a doctor and a mom who was a nurse meant that I could never get away with pretending to be sick so that I could stay home from school. As a teenager I loved the show ER. I would watch it and inevitably either Mom or Dad would make their way into the living room. Within minutes they would be offering commentary on how inaccurate the show was. "Oh, you would NEVER do that in an ER," and so on.

I had to ban them from watching with me so I could enjoy the drama in ignorant bliss of its many health code violations. I gained a whole new appreciation for the health-care world when I faced the second surgery I mentioned in chapter one.

My surgeon's expertise enabled him to spot something on a video chat that a local physician had originally dismissed as unproblematic. I had contracted a serious infection after the initial surgery to remove part of my thyroid. Apparently this was a pretty rare occurrence that could have caused irreversible damage, even death, if my doctor had not caught it.

After that second operation I spent five days in the hospital with one primary purpose: to identify the exact type of infection so an effective course of treatment could be given. Every day they would draw my blood and test it to see how it was responding to the different antibiotics they were giving me. By day four they finally felt confident the exact strain had been identified. I was sent home with medication that would attack the specific source of the infection.

There is not one blanket medication that can effectively treat all types of infections. From the outside looking in, it was obvious I was sick. But determining how sick I was and what was causing the sickness required finding the source. It required trial and error, which finally produced success. The trials we go through are a lot like that infection. To effectively navigate trials in life we need to know where they are coming from. We need to identify their source because that will tell us the best course of treatment.

CONSIDER IT JOY

At that time, sourcing my trials was a new concept for me. I began studying the book of James and how James, one of Jesus' disciples, instructed people to consider trials "a joyful thing." Trials are hard. We call them trials because they try us. They test our resolve and expose what we are really made of. Joy is a word that hardly ever comes to mind when we are going through trials. If there is any joy connected to them it is often playing hard to get.

Yet here we are being instructed by God to find joy in our trials. We are told to tap into the hidden places and mine out the gold we are promised is awaiting us. This is one of those places in scripture where the tension is thick. The words sound pretty but there is a big disconnect between reading and doing.

Here is the truth that I believe James is tapping into: Not all trials are the same. The source of the trial is important. Once we identify the source, we can approach the trial with a specific plan of action that will not only bring about the desired outcome of the trail, but also expose the hidden joy within it. The challenge is to identify the source of each trial by digging deeper and looking within.

The outward effects of a hard season are pretty straight forward. Life gets hard, we get stressed, anxious, depressed, angry or hurt. We instinctively start trying to cope with these feelings by going to our comfort place. Maybe for you it's binge eating, binge watching, binge smoking, binge sleeping, or another manner of trying to get full on something that feels good. Does the coping every really help? Not really. So why do we do it? Why do we keep feeding our internal needs with external attempts at a moment of gratification?

I propose we stop falling prey to our hardships by breaking the cycle of self-indulgence and its attempt to numb reality. In his brilliant book "The Good Fight Of Faith," Alan Vincent suggests a word picture that has stuck with me. In the scene two men are fighting in a boxing match. One fighter is clearly on the offensive, and he is repeatedly punching the other fighter square in the jaw. The second fighter does little to defend himself. The crowd yells at him to dodge the punches and protect himself, all the while probably thinking he is an idiot.

Vincent suggests how ridiculous the second fighter appears in this scenario. Now imagine you have insider information that this second fighter made a pre-fight agreement that he would receive $10,000 for every punch he could take standing up. That insight would change everything. You'd go from yelling at the second fighter to becoming his biggest fan. The shouts would change to chants assuring him he can take another one. "It will all be worth it! Yeah! You got another hit! How about one more? Get back up! Woo-Hoo!"

Perspective is everything. We are like the second fighter. Having new insight gives us new strength to stand strong when we are getting slammed by life. It is possible to discover this insight in every trial we go through. It starts when we find ourselves in a hard place and yet we quickly begin to see why the hardship is there in the first place. What does it want to do for us? What better version of ourselves will emerge because we are going through this?

Now that we see it clearly, we know exactly how to navigate it. As we navigate the difficulty, a strange thing starts to happen. We begin to notice joy. That joy actually makes us thankful for the difficulty. Sounds ideal, right?!? Let's get practical so we can make that our reality.

3 TYPES OF TRIALS

Let's look at three sources that trials and hardships come from. The first kind of trial is the kind that is actually an attack from the demonic world. Next, we have trials that are the unfortunate consequences of bad decisions we have made. Finally, there are the trials that come from God Himself. Each of these types of trials have specific goals they are trying to accomplish. The key to your breakthrough is understanding what is going on under the surface.

This first type of trial is the most straight forward, and we talked about it in the previous chapter. Let's briefly revisit it from another angle. These spiritual warfare trials are orchestrated by the devil as he attempts to sever our relationship with God. When the enemy comes against you he is out for blood, and everything in your life can become collateral damage.

Collateral damage, by definition, is injury inflicted on something other than an intended target. This whole spiritual battle around us is about the enemy trying to sabotage everything God values and created. Remember that satan hates us because we have the one thing he will never have. We are God's children with direct access to His presence. God is his intended target and you are the collateral damage.

As much as this type of trial may affect you, it's not actually about you. It's an all out assault on God and the presence of God in you. Sometimes, you and I get caught in the crossfire of this battle, and when that happens our lives end up being the enemy's battlefield. As we grow as sons and daughters of God these trials become easier to expose and overcome.

When you find yourself in a trial that is a spiritual attack, you have the authority to rebuke the enemy and tell him to leave. There is no reason to let him linger in your life. If you are not getting breakthrough as you stand firm and resist what the enemy is doing, do not give up! Often there can be a subtle lie that has been believed that has opened the door to the enemy, allowing him to linger. Holy Spirit will help you as you seek the Lord. Jesus wants these attacking trials gone as much as you do.

Deliverance ministry can be a helpful tool in these situations as well. Find someone who has battled and won against these types of trials. Ask them to pray for you and let Holy Spirit help you get rid of the lies or oppression the enemy might be subjecting you to.

This second kind of trial is the most confusing. It is the type of trial that is caused by our own actions. We want to believe that our actions do not cause reactions, but that is not always the case. Receiving forgiveness for our sins does not necessarily nullify the natural consequences of our actions.

Pretend you are someone who has stolen some money. You can be forgiven for stealing the money but despite being forgiven, you still have an obligation to pay it back. In this scenario, the burden of having to repay such a large sum of money might feel like an attack on your finances.

However, knowing the whole story makes it clear that repayment is not actually a demonic attack on your finances. It is a burden caused by your own actions. This is why knowing the source is important. In relationships we can be forgiven for saying something hurtful or damaging to a loved one, but the effects of those words do not disappear right away. There are trials that we face that are direct consequences of the choices that we make.

Marriage is one of the places this often happens. Sometimes the strain in our relationship is the trial we are facing. The cause of the strain can often be traced back to an argument or hurtful moment where trust was broken. If we approach this type of trial in the same manner as a demonic attack we are not likely to get much breakthrough. Instead, we have to take responsibility for our actions and be willing to make things right if we can.

Another way to approach this type of trial is the principle of sowing and reaping found in Galatians 6:8. The choices that we make matter. We will eventually reap what we sow. We cannot be consistently mean to people and then become surprised when people are mean to us. You should not be surprised when you hear people are gossiping about you if you have been gossiping about other people. There is only one course of action in these situations. Repentance.

We must repent for our actions and the consequences of our choices. We must take responsibility for any harm we have done and allow God to deal with us as He sees necessary. I think these trials are helpful for us because they often allows us to see what it is like in someone else's shoes. There is no better way to gain perspective than to experience something you have done to other people firsthand. I do not mean to say this in a harsh manner, but it is the truth.

Sometimes we feel it is so easy to judge someone for their choices. We talk behind their backs, spread gossip, or feel good about ourselves because "we would never do that". At times, God will allow us to go through those very same situations so we can see that we don't actually know what we would do or how we would respond until we're in that situation ourselves.

The third source of trials are the ones that come from God Himself. Sometimes it gets uncomfortable when we talk about God bringing people into hard seasons of trial and testing. It doesn't mean that God is not pleased with us. In fact, when we are tested and tried by God we should be excited. God never sets us up to fail so He can laugh at our expense, or delight in our weakness. He will, however, lead us into seasons that expose the weak points of our faith.

We see this clearly in the book of James.

> *"Be assured and understand that the trial and proving of your faith bring out endurance and steadfastness and patience."*
> *(James 1:3 AMP)*

These trials are not to show you how weak you are but to show you how to become strong in Him.

> *"In this you rejoice, though now for a little while, if necessary, you have been grieved by various trials, so that the tested genuineness of your faith—more precious than gold that perishes though it is tested by fire—may be found to result in praise and glory and honor at the revelation of Jesus Christ."*
> *(1 Peter 1:6-7 ESV)*

When God is the source of your trial there is no manner of rebuking that will help you. Life becomes about enduring and discovering as we let God work on the thing He is wanting to work on. These trials are invitations to surrender again to the lordship of Jesus.

You can see how important it is to know the point of origin for what you are going through. These different sources need different approaches. There is purpose in your trial if you look for it. Learn to lean on God. Jesus gave us His Holy Spirit to help us navigate hard seasons in life. Holy Spirit comforts us, encourages us, and equips us for success.

No matter the type of trial you find yourself in the middle of, you are not there alone. If it's from the enemy, resist and rebuke it. Find joy in the victory and the strength that is added to you now that you have victory on that battlefield.

If it's from your own actions, take responsibility and ask Jesus how He wants you to proceed. Find joy in becoming a mature son or daughter of God. If it is from God, surrender. Find joy in the fact that He is growing you up.

When God initiates these seasons we have the choice to work with God or resist Him. Ideally, as soon as we recognize an area for growth, we also see His provision to make that growth a reality. All too often we fight against growth, which makes the frustration of the circumstance last much longer than necessary.

It takes some effort on our part not to resist His correction or wince in frustration when our heart is exposed before Him. It takes maturity to trust that He is with us while we are growing and developing into an even more Christ-like version of ourselves. When God leads us into a difficult season it's because He wants to show us what is really inside our hearts. Once we know what's really in there He can help us remove the parts that are not like Him.

TRIALS VS. TESTS

Are trials and tests the same thing? Not necessarily. In my house we don't give much accolade for school grades. We encourage our kids to go for A's but we look at report cards and tests as tools that expose the truth about what they are learning. The grades serve as a tool to measure learning, not a measure of someone's worth as a person.

Tests from the Lord are designed to do the same thing. They show us what we know to be true and help us to put it into practice. As a preacher, I regularly experience this when God is leading me into a revelation that I will teach to others. The revelations are fascinating and empowering. I often feel an adrenaline-like high as I explore His truths being revealed to me from the Bible. But my learning and revelation must be coupled with practicality or it is fruitless. Knowing the word and not doing the word is a dangerous thing for a believer.

I can usually bank on the fact that God will orchestrate a set of circumstances where I will be set up to put the new revelation I am learning into practice. If I am learning about honor I can expect someone to come into my life that does not outwardly deserve honor. I get to practice what I am learning by honoring them anyway.

If I am learning about staying focused on the peace of God it would not come as a surprise if I found my life becoming disrupted. Why? Because I know the disruption offers me the chance to put legs to the thoughts about peace. Do you see the pattern? These are tests from the Lord.

Our American obsession with perfection is so counterintuitive to the life Jesus calls us to. How can we really learn if we are expecting ourselves to get it right the first time and every time afterwards? The main purpose of these tests are for us to see how we are doing. What is God teaching us in this season of our lives? Are we learning it well? Is it sinking into our hearts? Are we giving these new thoughts enough attention so our brains are adapting around this new reality? Or do we have more learning and practicing to do?

In my opinion, the bulk of our tests and trials come from the Lord. He created the system of resistance and growth because it works best with the way He designed us as humans. The resistance is not meant to be a sign that God is not present. It is not meant to be a deterrent for us either. Resistance is an opportunity for us to practice our faith and what we believe. It allows us to build stronger highways of thoughts and patterns for our subconscious.

This system was developed based upon an understanding that many of us do not yet have and that might be why it is hard for us to find the joy. All of the things we face in life are opportunities to strengthen our relationship with God. Life is designed to be lived from the perspective that we are always connected to Him. We are not working our way through life trying to win His approval or get Him to notice us.

If we know that we are accepted and pleasing to our Father God, we don't have to try to prove ourselves anymore. When we realize that we have nothing to prove, we can partner with God through the trials that are before us. It truly does become a joy, just like James says, because we see where He is working in and through our lives. It becomes obvious why He wants to grow a specific area of our lives. We become free to stop resisting Him. We stop being afraid that God is embarrassed by our progress. We learn to find Him regardless of our circumstances.

chapter eight

HE CALLED IT LOVE

One of my favorite songs is the Bonnie Taylor classic, "I Need a Hero." I love to crank up the volume and dance around like a maniac. I remember doing this very thing one day in my kitchen with my kids. I was twirling from here to there, dancing my heart out. We were all giggling and having a great time. I belted out the chorus, "I need a hero! I'm holding out for a hero 'til the end of the night…"

Suddenly I realized how true those words were. I wanted a hero to come and do the hard work of building my faith for me. I wanted a knight on a white horse to ride in and fix all of my problems. Truth be told, there are still days this sounds nice!

Just yesterday I was thinking about how it is so annoying

that you can't hire someone to exercise for you. We can hire people to clean our house, cook, shop, watch our kids, and everything else…except we can't hire someone to build our muscles. Sure, we can hire a personal trainer but we're still the ones doing the lifting.

In reality, we don't really need a hero who can come and do everything for us. In fact, if we had a hero, our faith wouldn't be nearly as strong. The strength of our faith is revealed through the process of using it. If someone could swoop in and fix our brokenness we would not be strong enough to navigate our future trials.

Some of us love playing the damsel in distress. What we don't realize is that the damsel never gets the pleasure and joy of living a well-built life. She is completely dependent on everyone else. Her wants and desires are constantly shelved because she has to take what she can get from others.

God did not create us to be in need of constant rescuing. Of course He will always be our rescuer but He is more than that. We have to allow ourselves to mature and grow. If we are being honest with ourselves, how often do we resist the cycle of growth that God has put in place for us? The unfortunate truth is that no one else is responsible for the state of our faith. What we believe is entirely up to us.

Facing the loss of my son and threat of cancer forced me to take a hard look at what I believed. The subtle idea that God would snap His fingers and suddenly make everything better just couldn't hold up. It didn't work. There was no short cut out of my despair. There was only hard work. This is where we sink or swim.

Are you reading this right now and thinking that you chose to sink? It is not too late to start swimming! For me, I knew it was time to rise. Truthfully, I didn't want to rise. I wanted to wallow. I wanted to become invisible so that no one would see me struggling to make sense out of my life.

If I could do it then you certainly can too. It is time for you to rise. You might stand up battered and broken. You might stand up not really sure if you mean it. Stand nonetheless. Do not let life sink you.

Whatever thing you have been going through was powerful. No doubt you will be different because you have experienced it. But different is not the same thing as dead. Different is not the same thing as stalled out and off track. You can move forward despite what you have gone through. Will it be hard? For sure. Will it be worth it? Absolutely.

Every time we face a crossroads concerning what we believe about God we have an opportunity to rise up and take the reins of our faith. We get to decide if we will allow God to do a good work in us or if we will resist Him. But there is one thing we have to set straight before I can show you how to rise when you've gotten comfy in your wallowing hole. God is not in control.

GOD IS NOT IN CONTROL

I vividly remember sitting across from a friend and talking about life when she said these shocking words: "Have you realized that God is actually not in control?" The words cut me. At first it felt like blasphemy. I mean, I was in the junior high youth group choir in the 90s singing the Point of Grace hit song "God is in Control." I knew every word of that song, but I never once searched the Bible to see if it was true. I was left stunned, challenged, and perplexed.

In the years since that conversation I have come to fully believe that statement. God is not in control, but He is absolutely sovereign. That statement does not imply He is at a distance. What it does imply is that things happen that were not in God's plan. There are a multitude of scriptures that affirm God's sovereign nature, His nearness, and His ability to turn all things for good for those that are in Jesus. There are none that firmly state He is in control.

We serve the most incredible God. In His amazing wisdom He created the world with one major loophole. We call it free will. He called it love. You get to choose Him or not. He will not force you to choose Him, His ways, or His ideas. What this means is that you have the ability to choose something He would not choose. You are also susceptible to experience something that is not in His plan for your life.

God has chosen not to control you. It was a deliberate choice to make you in His image…and He is not controlling. He has the freedom of choice and He gave us that freedom so we would bear His image accurately. He was not looking to create pawns on a chess board. He wanted people with a mind of their own who would choose to love and pursue Him. Of course He is fully capable of taking control, but God is not interested in controlling you and everything that happens to you.

I think we find comfort in saying God is in control. It's like plausible deniability or a way to categorize an experience that defies our comprehension. The problem with this is not only that the Bible fails to mention that God is in control, but all throughout the Bible there are situations that were seemingly OUT of God's control.

Eve eating the fruit, a handful of evil kings in Israel setting up demonic worship structures that led the people away from God, Joseph getting sold into slavery, and David lusting over Bathsheba are just a few examples of times when God was obviously not controlling the situation.

Just looking at the world around us today we will quickly see that God is not in control of everything that is going on. Complete control was never on His mind when He went about creating our world. God is not in control, but He is heavily involved. This is the structure He created and found good. He created the system of the world to function such that He is as involved in our lives as we allow Him to be.

This notion of God being "in control" sounds good to the person who has given Him the control. That doesn't apply to everyone and it certainly does not apply to every situation. For me, I told Jesus a long time ago that I was making a pretty good mess of my life. I asked Him to take control and He did…but that was my choice. Even today He is not interacting with me in a controlling manner. He will point things out that He thinks I need to change. Then it becomes entirely my choice if I want to partner with Him or not.

Before we explore this concept further I want to stop and address tragedies and abuse for those that have endured them. I will not attempt to explain why this happened to you. I have experienced some of this as well and I can say it is one of the greatest mysteries in life. I can tell you that there are things in life that are beyond God's control. I know that God was not, and is not, happy this has happened to you. He takes no delight in the hurt of others and He will get justice in this life or the next.

Consider the Garden of Eden in Genesis chapters 1-3. God purposefully planted the tree of knowledge of good and evil in the garden so that humans would be able to choose to love Him. It was planted right in plain view. Why? So we would be free to choose to love Him or not.

Genesis 2:9 says that the tree of the knowledge of good and evil was planted in the middle of the garden right next to the tree of life. This is what I call the danger zone. Then, in an even more baffling move, God gives the most basic instruction of all time. Let's look at Genesis 2:16-17:

> *"And the Lord God commanded the man, saying, You may freely eat of every tree of the garden; But of the tree of the knowledge of good and evil and blessing and calamity you shall not eat, for in the day that you eat of it you shall surely die."*
> *(Genesis 2:16-17, AMP)*

That's all the Bible tells us God said about that horribly bad tree that possessed eternity-shaking power. God was not wringing His hands in worry wondering how and when His precious kids would disobey Him. He trusted. He loved. He empowered. He released them to choose freely.

If it was me, I would have struggled to say those instructions so simply, let alone with a non-manipulative tone. Knowing how destructive the first sin would be to the world, I probably would have planted the tree about a four day walk from the farthest edge of the garden. God planted that tree in the middle of the buffet line. There was no "out of sight, out of mind" happening in that garden.

Again, if I was planting that tree and handing that garden over to my precious babies, I would have enforced the instructions with a little more gusto. Something like, "Adam, PLEASE don't eat from that tree. Not only will you die on that day but you'll mess up the whole world FOREVER! That tree is terrible, don't go near it, don't touch it, don't smell it, don't even acknowledge it! If you love me at all just leave that tree alone."

I would harp on it so much that there would be no interest in that tree by the time I was done…but that would be manipulation. God knew what He was doing when He put that tree right in the middle of the Garden next to the tree of life. He was giving Adam a fair choice with no strings attached.

He desires pure trust and love and He knows that it can never be established when there is control and manipulation. By placing the tree front and center, it was as if God was saying, "Love me or not, either way I have already settled that you are the focus of *my* love. And if you choose to not obey me, I will still love you anyway."

This is so fascinating and empowering. It is amazing that

the God of everything would willingly subject Himself to this system in an effort to receive that which He longs for most. He longs for us to have the ability to represent Him. He pines for our worship that is not coerced. He adores it when we freely give Him our adoration and our unsolicited love.

God never wanted to be in control. He wanted to be in a relationship. He has no intention of manipulating us into doing something we don't want to do. I think we simply are not capable of understanding how much our freely given worship, love, and adoration moves His heart. It is such a powerful feeling to Him that He was willing to risk one of His loved ones not choosing Him in order to receive it.

Even today, He is not in control of our lives but He is in our lives and He has promised to be with us no matter what. We get to choose how involved we want Him to be.

I love this analogy of a landlord. A good landlord would not come inside the renter's house uninvited and make himself at home with the renter's things. He would ask permission even though he owns the home. The same is true with God and us. We are His, and yet He chooses to wait to enter until we give Him permission. He lets us engage with life however we want. He LOVES to be involved but He chooses not to force Himself on us. He will not demand our love and attention. He refuses to manipulate or control us. He simply stands at the door and knocks.

GOD, I GIVE YOU CONTROL

Is God in control? That is really up to you. You can give

Him control of your life and I hope you do. But you need to recognize not everyone has done that. Because of this, there are things that will happen that were not in God's plan. Thankfully, when we have brought God into all the areas of our lives He does what He does best. He takes all of those things that happened outside of His plan and He works them out for our good.

Ok, back to the garden. God's trust was broken as Eve and Adam took that fateful bite from the tree. Genesis chapter 3 tells us how sin then entered the world. Now there was a blemish on the pure hearts of Adam and Eve that had to be dealt with so that their relationship with God could remain intact.

Father God had to remove them from the Garden of Eden but He did not remove them from Himself. He did not turn His back in disappointment, nor did He distance Himself in a passive aggressive attempt to cause shame. He was so committed to their relationship that even after they sinned, He helped them to make clothes and to learn the skills they needed to survive outside the garden. Then He did something we are still processing today…He initiated the system of death.

The garden had the power of longevity. Adam and Eve, and their subsequent descendants, were originally designed to live incredibly long, if not immortal, lives. Humankind was designed and created for eternal communion with God.

Ecclesiastes 3:11 says that God put eternity into the hearts of man. Like a homing device, God placed within his creation the longing for eternal communion with Him. Seeing Adam and Eve's sin and the effects it would take on their bodies, He made a perplexing decision to take these people who were hardwired for eternity and place them in a world where death would exist.

We are designed to live forever. Not because of some potion, special diet, or the fountain of youth, but because we are made in God's image and He is everlasting. His intention is to be united with us forever. It is hardwired into us but we are living in a world that cannot support that. I suspect this is why we struggle with the finality of death so severely. It's almost as if we don't have the ability to process it. Maybe, in fact, we don't.

If you are someone who has come face to face with death or lost a dear loved one, I am so sorry. I am sorry you are now facing the impossible task of making sense of a nonsensical reality. You may not be able to wrap your mind around it and that's ok. That's normal. I have found there is only one place I can go to process death and it is God's heart. Father God, Jesus, and Holy Spirit designed death. They believed it was necessary on this side of the Garden of Eden and they are the best, most capable source of comfort for your grief.

If that totally sounds morbid, please understand that I am not really suggesting we celebrate death or darkness. I am suggesting that there is a way through grief and it is found in connection to a God who may not have had control over your situation but who can lead you through it.

Our tendency in grief is to blame God because we think

He is the one inflicting all our pain. We know He is the only one who could have prevented it and yet it still happened. The terrible truth is that when we blame we back up. We put up walls and boundaries. Then we end up distancing ourselves from the only one who can actually help.

Holy Spirit, I pray for every reader dealing with grief right now. I pray you give them fresh eyes to see where you are at work in this situation. I pray for open ears to be able to hear your voice leading them through their pain. I pray they feel your nearness. As they cry and feel and hurt, I pray they feel you crying and feeling and hurting alongside of them. Jesus, do what only you can do. Bring breakthrough, healing, and hope. Amen.

Embracing the perspective that God is not in control can help you move forward. First, we recognize that waiting for our knight in shining armor is not productive. Second, we begin to understand that God was not happily inflicting our pain. Nor was He sitting silently indifferent as we endured the traumas of our lives. Finally, we are empowered to discover what God will do as we invite Him in and give Him permission to make our ashes into something beautiful.

chapter nine

YOUR GREATEST BATTLE IN LIFE

We have explored several areas of struggle so far, but the words of this chapter are dedicated to shining light on what I believe is our greatest battle in life. Hopefully I will inspire you to wield your sword and get your fight on. I want to encourage you to rise up and rush to the battlefield with victory already in hand.

What's the battlefield? Your understanding of your place as God's child. As I leaned into our Father's heart to write this chapter I heard Him whisper something specific to you. He knew you would be reading this and He wanted you to read these words.

Dear One,

I truly cannot get enough of you. You bring me SO much joy! I am so enamored with you. You may not realize it, but you are special to me. It doesn't matter what you've done, I am here for you. I want nothing more than to be close to you. Don't clean yourself up for me. Don't try to put on your best clothes and fix your hair so I will think you're some hot shot...because I already do. I already think more highly of you than you could imagine. You are mine. My child. The joy of my heart. Set aside your striving to impress me and be who I already made you to be. That's the you I love the most.

Love,
Dad

All of life is about connection to Father God. From the beginning He was longing for a family. Family is supposed to be the place where you let your hair down, put your pjs on, and be your truest self. When God began to create people this is what He had in mind. Closeness in both proximity and heart connection. I think He envisioned lazy Saturday mornings where you eat waffles and just enjoy being together. He envisioned going out on the town and laughing until you cry. He envisioned being right there for you when heartache comes.

This vision is poison to the demonic realm. They can't have that anymore. Remember, all the forces of darkness were once forces of light. The accuser, formerly known as Lucifer, was the lead worshiper of God before he rose up against Him and was cast out (Ezekiel 28:16). The fate of the demonic realm is sealed now. They have been eternally removed from the family of God forever.

The kingdom of darkness knows the secret to a thriving life. True thriving cannot exist without embracing our place as a son or daughter of God. You can be saved and still be distant from Father God. You can know theology, pray, and even see miracles, all while not understanding your place as His child. But you cannot have true freedom in your heart and soul without knowing your identity. The enemy knows this and he works tirelessly to get you away from the connected place Father God has created for you.

Think about that. All the attacks and all the trials have one agenda...putting distance between you and God. Their aim is to stop His plan for your life by twisting truth to make you work for the approval He has already freely given. Their goal is to distort reality in an effort to get you to withdraw from God's presence. The enemy throws obstacles in your way hoping they will cause your heart to breed bitterness and anger towards the one person who can help you the most.

We are all God's children, every one of us, whether we choose to acknowledge it or not. Throughout the New Testament we are referred to as sons, which was a word translated from the Greek word huios. Huios refers to (figuratively) anyone sharing the same nature as their Father. It also refers to having a legal right to the Father's inheritance.

Whether you are male or female you are a huios, or son of God. It took me a minute to get used to being a woman who is also a son. However, verses like Galatians 4:6 and Romans 8:14 point to the nature of a child and they are inclusive of both men and women. It is my personal conviction that the journey of embracing our place as a son (or daughter) of God is the greatest journey of our lives. It is the hardest as well.

Why is it so hard? Because the enemy will stop at nothing to keep us from walking in that identity. It is so threatening to him on so many levels. When I see myself a son of God I am not thinking in terms of masculinity but in terms of proximity. The Creator God has given me the right to be close to Him. Why, then, would I allow myself to stay at a distance?

I wish I could accurately explain the way it feels for this revelation of my sonship to be solidified in my heart. It has become so effortless to trust Him, even in hard and confusing situations. There is a completeness I now feel in the depths of my soul. So many years were wasted being frustrated with God and not understanding His ways or how He truly felt about me.

SONSHIP AND THE ORPHAN SPIRIT

There is an identity called sonship that God leads us towards. This proverbial line in the sand marks the full embodiment of our place as God's child. It's not just about salvation; it marks our place in the family of God. Once we step across that line we are changed forever.

The process requires seeing the line, understanding what the line is all about, and doing the hard work of uprooting any false beliefs to get over that line. That's not to say there will not be trials and struggles on the other side of the line. But the approach to those things becomes completely different once the line has been crossed.

Sonship is about so much more than being able to quote bible verses or singing "Good, Good Father" and meaning it. It is connection, depth, how we live and see the world, how we think, and it involves a lot of trust. It is learning to trust that God is really a good Dad, especially when that doesn't feel true. Trust is built through experience and it takes time.

Real trust and assurance of God's goodness becomes forged over seasons of testing and seeing results. As we put our faith and trust in Him, even when it feels scary, we are taking steps to grow that relationship. We are making deposits into the metaphorical joint banking account we share with God. Over time we can see how faithful and good He truly is. It's so much easier to admire God from a distance so we don't feel the pain of hurt and disappointment if things go sideways.

The number one thing someone walking in their sonship does is communicate. Two way dialogue is essential to understanding God's heart and getting that same heart into us. This process of this battle for sonship is not a quick one but it is so worthwhile. In fact, you are on that journey right now! Every one of us is on this journey. Now it's time to start engaging in the process so you can get across that line and thrive.

Many years ago I had a friend give me a set of sermons on a CD with the words "the orphan spirit" scribbled on top of them. This was back when burning songs and teachings onto CDs to share with friends was a normal thing. I was in a season of life where I was beginning to learn about God as a Father. More accurately, I was learning about God as my Father. I mean, I knew He was real, and I knew He was important. I just hadn't learned a lot about Him.

Pretty much my entire Christian journey had been about Jesus. Even when I would read the Old Testament I saw God as a God. I would envision Him as a deity – a force not to be reckoned with. In my mind He was slightly far off but very much opinionated. It was beyond my scope to see Him as a Father to His people.

I had heard a few sermons on the topic of the Father heart of God and they were moving but there was always a disconnect for me. I just did not know how to see God any differently. Yes, I called Him "Father" from time to time, but "Father" was a stand-offish term. Kind of like how Michael Banks would speak to his father in Mary Poppins. More focused on respect and reverence than relationship. The reality was I was always a little nervous about what He might do or say when I addressed Him.

When my friend gave me those CDs I was intrigued. They were messages from a man who had encountered God as a Dad and it changed him forever. It ended up changing me as well. I use the word encounter because that is exactly what happened to him and to me.

An encounter is when you are going about your life one way and then, BAM, you run right smack into God and you are forever changed. Isn't this the theme of the New Testament too? People would find their way to Jesus, interact with Him, and become changed forever. He still does this today. I assume you have encountered Jesus in some way in your life.

Did you know you can encounter Father God in the same way? You might be thinking that you don't want to. We have a tendency to approach Father God like we approach our earthly fathers. It is hard not to project our opinion of our earthly dad onto our heavenly one. They are not the same. Even if you have a great dad, your Father God is better.

Ephesians chapter 3 tells us that Father God is a perfect father. Think about that. What do you think a perfect father is like? Part of the sonship process is deliberately refusing to see Father God in the same way as your earthly dad, whether good or bad.

That is no easy feat. As I listened to those CDs, the speaker began to introduce the concept of an orphan spirit or orphan mentality. This is not a spirit we get delivered from but rather a mentality that must be replaced. Orphans have a specific way of thinking. They have no one to meet their needs so they develop a world-view where they become the one meeting their own needs.

The two primary needs every orphan has are provision and protection. No one is providing them with food, clothes, shelter, bathing, shoes, etc. No one is responsible for their protection either. Their safety and emotional well-being is entirely up to them.

This is not the way we are designed to live. Yet, spiritually speaking, many of us are in this exact spot. We think we are spiritual orphans who have to look out for ourselves, provide for ourselves, and protect ourselves. We struggle to connect with God as our Dad because we can't get past all the ways we have been living alone for so long.

We are like little orphan Annie after Daddy Warbucks brings her into his home for the first time. We may be glad to be there, but even though we may be feeling a little more safe, we still aren't yet connected to the dad who is providing it all. Like Annie, we are still looking out for ourselves and our own well-being. Just because someone is located in a father's house does not take away the orphan thinking.

Annie, like all of us, had to come to love her new dad. If a sequel was ever made I imagine it would be the story of Annie learning to let go of her orphan thinking and embrace what it means to now be a daughter. We would see her learning how to let go of thoughts that are not helpful. We would see her learning how to trust her new dad. She would have some wrestling to do.

How do you know if you have orphan thinking in you? Take a moment to answer these questions honestly:

- Do you often feel alone?
- Do you struggle to feel at home in the presence of God?
- Do you find yourself shutting down your emotions to protect yourself from being hurt?
- Do you often feel like people have abandoned you?

- Is it hard to trust God for financial needs?
- Do you regularly feel your spiritual needs are entirely your responsibility?

These are some of the thoughts that come from an orphan mentality. I found myself saying yes to every single one of these when I began this process. Most of us are conditioned to live life alone. We became conditioned through the accumulation of times when we tried to trust God only to feel it didn't work. We believed God for a miracle He didn't perform. Perhaps we tried to do the right thing and trust other people only to become hurt in the process.

I want you to know there is a different and better way. As I came face to face with my orphan mentality I felt equally frustrated and justified. I was frustrated because I knew enough Christian culture to know that I shouldn't close myself off from God. But I felt justified because the list of moments when I believed He failed me was so long.

There were moments as a child when I was mistreated and abused. Trying to approach God as my dad was opening a huge can of worms. How could you let that happen? Where were you when I needed you? This moment affected me forever and you just stood by and did nothing!?!

My process of undoing the orphan thinking began to touch every area of my life. I am not going to lie to you. It was really hard to sort through the thoughts I was so convinced were true and see my life from a new perspective. Amazingly, every time I brought a different hurt to God as my Dad He would do something that floored me. He would heal it.

It was like I would hand God a memory or thought process and we would start to talk about it. It was not just me unloading angry words into the sky. I would ask about it and He would actually respond to me. He would show me His perspective and it was so incredible. I could never have come up with that on my own. He would give me His perspective and I got to choose if I wanted to accept it or not. Once I did, it started to become my perspective. As the days turned into weeks I noticed how much closer I was coming to that sonship line.

One such moment I was sitting in my car in an empty parking lot. I know, I'm weird. I just love to connect with God in my car. I think it's because I feel private and have little distraction when I'm sitting behind the wheel. Anyway, I was worshiping and using my imagination to connect with God. Sometimes God interrupts those daydreams and speaks something amazing. This was one of those times.

I began to picture myself sitting beside this really beautiful little creek in a serene field. I was pretending I was really sitting there while I prayed and talked to God. Father God walked up to me and stuck His hand into my chest and pulled something off of my heart. I asked Him what He removed.

"I am taking guilt and shame off of you," He said gently. "But Lord, I don't think I struggle with guilt and shame," I responded. "You do," He replied. "You do not feel you are worthy of being in my presence and you feel guilty about connecting with me on such a deep level." His words struck me as I realized how true they were. "I'm taking care of that," He said with a smile.

Something changed in me. I felt lighter…more free. I began to see how true those words were. How I had felt so unworthy of His love, and so undeserving of His blessings.

This next part might be a little hard to believe, but I am telling you the truth. I was healed in that interaction. Something that started as a daydream turned into an encounter that changed my life. The most incredible part is that He can and will do this for you too!

LET GOD BE YOUR DAD

What would your life look like if you knew you were at peace with yourself and who God has made you to be? How would you feel about yourself if you didn't think you were a failure, a disappointment, or a burden? What kind of pressure could you let go of if you truly believed God was going to take care of your needs financially, and even provide for your wants too?

This is what life is like when you come to know God as Father. He is the ultimate Daddy who wants to play with you and push you higher on the swing. He loves to sit down and have tea parties and wrestle fights. He wants to listen... to whatever you want to say. Want to have deep talks? He loves those too.

God is the kind of Dad who sees you are having a bad day and pats His lap as an invitation for you to climb on up. Once you're situated, He will play with your hair and listen as you tell Him all about whatever is bothering you. Need to vent for a moment? No problem. He is the kind of Dad who wants to be involved in all the details, however much you're willing to share with Him.

As He listens to you share your heart, He stores those words as precious secrets. He is the kind of Dad who doesn't go bringing up your failures to other people and He has no intention of embarrassing you. He listens intently and has this incredible ability to spot what's really at the heart of why you're hurting. Then, if you let Him, He will speak kindly right into that very place.

His voice doesn't thunder with the sound of frustration or the accusation that you just can't get your life together. His voice is tender, calm, and filled with the assurance of love. God knows that what you're feeling in any given moment may not represent who you really are. He does not define you by your feelings. You may be having a bad day but He knows it is just that - a singular bad day. And God knows that things can get better tomorrow.

As He speaks, Father God's voice brings a comfort and a power that only He can bring. You can tell yourself a great piece of advice and it will ring true in your spirit. Heck, it might even have a measure of power in it. But when God speaks it, those words are the words of life itself. Within them is the power to overcome. God's words release the strength that allows us to rise above our feelings and every other hurdle in our way.

Father God is so tremendously patient with us, kind towards us, and just a big teddy bear of love for us. He's a papa bear, too, and He is careful to bring justice wherever it is needed. Did I mention that He is also the fun Dad? He LOVES to run around with you, take you on roller coasters and buy you the fried Twinkie at the fair just for the fun of it!

His arms are always open ready to receive you. There is always celebration in His heart. His presence is filled with so much peace, joy, and a love that is power itself. I wonder if you have experienced these parts of the Father heart of God?

As I began to discover these attributes I felt as if I was getting saved all over again. The gospel became so much bigger than just my need to be "saved" from hell so I could go to heaven. It became the necessary act to deal with my sin so I could experience all the greatness of my Father God.

Even though I have a great dad named Larry, God is also my dad. I call Him "Dad" now and it's not weird to me anymore. I have encountered Him and have been changed forever. Want to know the best part? He wants that for you, too. Take a moment to read over those last few paragraphs again if you need to.

Father God is SO much more than the few qualities I have mentioned, but see if there are any of those attributes that you have not experienced for yourself? That's a great place to start. Notice any hesitation or hurt that rises up in you as you read those words. Make a note in the of those places. That might be an area of orphan thinking that God wants to deal with.

If you notice one of those areas you can use this helpful prayer tool:

God, I realize I find ______________________ to be an uncomfortable thought. I do not know how to experience you in this way. I give you permission to search my heart, and to speak to me about this. What do you want to say to me about this area of my life? How do you want to interact with me on this?

After praying this prayer take a moment to quiet your heart and listen. God may show you a picture. His response may come as a thought. He may play a little movie in your imagination to help you understand Him more. Write down how He responds even if it feels silly or too simple. Ask the Lord for discernment to help you know if you are hearing from God. Remember that He is more eager to connect with you than you can imagine!

chapter ten

HIDING IN PLAIN SIGHT

The Lord wants you to be an integrated person. Being integrated means that what you believe and how you live are intertwined. For many of us, there is a disconnect between what we believe and our ability to live out those beliefs on a practical level.

For example, we may read the truth in Hebrews 4:16 that we are invited to boldly approach God's throne at any time. But in real life, that belief doesn't dislodge the feeling that God wants to keep us at a distance. When the gap between our beliefs and the practicality of our lives grows too wide we stop moving forward.

Like a young child learning to do a split in socks on a tile floor, the farther apart their feet slide, the harder it is to stay standing. Knowing and doing are designed to be two feet of the same body. James 1:22 puts it this way, *"Do not merely listen to the word, and so deceive yourselves. Do what it says."* We are deceiving ourselves if we do not find ways to practice the Bible and live it out.

Integration is the process of building a bridge between what we know and how we act. When this bridge is built, we can effortlessly live out of a place of confidence in who God is and who He has said we are. We can know that God is good, believe that God is good, and approach and interact with Him in His goodness. Integration is the connectedness of thoughts, beliefs, and actions. When that bridge is broken, the insights and divine inspiration we are designed to receive cannot cross over into the practical areas of our lives.

I wrote this book because I wish I understood much earlier in my journey what had been made available to me through Jesus' ministry and ultimate sacrifice. I had regularly been in church since I was 11 years old and yet I did not understand the freedom that had been made available to me. Somehow I missed the memo that we are designed to be victorious people who do not live defeated lives.

You can overcome every single issue in your life because our God is THE God. He holds ALL the power. His ways are perfect. And He is totally and completely for you. He is always in a good mood and always ready to help. Knowing who He is and knowing the way He operates are two different things.

We have to learn His ways if we want to thrive. We have

to challenge ourselves to understand His why. Why does He do things the way He does? Those answers are not hiding in some cosmic mystery that you will never be able to understand. They are hiding in plain sight.

I assume you are familiar with the phrase,"The Lord works in mysterious ways." We typically say this when we don't understand something and we don't care enough to dig into the Bible to find answers. It is often a cop-out that has caused many believers to journey into a land of disconnectedness and not even know it.

The Old Testament is an ode to the ways of God. In these stories we see how God feels about His people, His Glory, the enemies of His people, and more. In the New Testament we see Jesus become the embodiment of God so that we can see Him much more clearly. His ways are not as much mysterious as they are specific. In their particularity they do not always make sense.

Truth be told, I don't think they are designed to make perfect sense to us as humans. God does not need our validation that His ways are good. In fact, He doesn't even need us to follow those ways. Yet He knows His way of living is the only way that gets us to the abundant life Jesus talked about.

Another central theme of the Old Testament is how humans have struggled since the beginning of time to submit to the ways of God. The people of Israel consistently went astray and chose to define their lives on their own terms. Against this backdrop of a nation struggling to embrace the ways of God several heroes emerged.

They were great men and women like Moses, Joshua, Deborah, David, and others. They all had one thing in common…they followed God's ways. Surrender and submission to God's ultimate will was the defining characteristic of each of the Old Testament heroes and they were elevated because of it.

Of course they were imperfect people, but they had discovered something important: The ways of God actually lead to the love of God. Jesus alluded to this in the book of Matthew:

> *"Take my yoke upon you, and learn from me, For I am gentle and lowly in heart, and you will find rest for your souls. For my yoke is easy, and my burden is light."*
> *(Matthew 11:29-30 ESV)*

In other words, God's ways will lead you to God's heart. His heart is everything you are looking for. Rest. Peace. Joy. Ease. They are all found in surrender to His ways.

On a very personal level I want to make a confession. I have never thrived more than in the place of complete surrender. Surrender is best defined as trust. As we willingly trust the Lord we give our self-control to Him and allow Him be in control of our lives.

So many of my struggles were about whether I truly trusted that God was good and had good plans for me. When I would feel the Holy Spirit's conviction to let go of something I held dear I would struggle to trust that He knew what was best for me. It sounds simple on paper but it was anything but simple. It was a yielding of power.

THE PICTURE OF SURRENDER

When my husband and I were processing and praying through the call to plant the church we now lead, I had an encounter with God that changed me. I was kneeling down in the presence of God as I was praying and telling the Lord He could have His way in my life. I prayed a prayer of surrender, one I had prayed many times before and since. As I knelt in His presence, I saw a picture of an angel come over to me and say, "This is not surrender. THIS is surrender." With those words the angel pulled my hands in front of me and I was face down and completely prostrate before the Lord.

I realized how hard it would be to direct my life from that posture and it became a defining moment for me. I laid down and stretched my hands completely in front of me as I saw in the picture and began to cry, "God, I have given you total control of my life because I trust you. The more I surrender to your ways the more I love you."

Whether you feel like it or not, surrender, love and trust are intertwined. Surrender is not abdication or indifference. It is not just throwing your hands up and not caring about your life anymore. It is a deliberate transfer of power, and a deliberate act of trust and love.

When we surrender to the Lord and His way for our lives it is an act of empowerment. We recognize our way will not get us to the best end goal so we come under the plan of the One whose way will. Sometimes surrender requires letting go of relationships and habits that stand in the way. Other times it is the moment we realize we are not capable of seeing the big picture of our lives.

Surrender is hardest when trust has been broken. Trust is not something we create on a whim instantaneously. True trust can not be conjured up out of nowhere. It is built over time and through risk. We build trust through shared experiences in marriage, family, with friends, our bosses and with the Lord. When we are invited into a moment of surrender it is an opportunity to build trust with God. Simply put, there is nothing more freeing than trusting God.

The more we surrender and watch how His way brings us into a better way of life, the more we trust. The more we trust, the more we are happy to surrender. It is a beautiful cycle of life. The ways of God are not hiding from you so you are left to your own demise. They are hiding in plain sight so you can decide if you want to be on the trust journey with Jesus.

As a spouse, God has a way for your marriage that will bring you into a deeper more incredible relationship. As a parent, God has a way for you to raise your child that will bring peace to your home and help them become all they are called by God to be. This applies to your job, your thought life, your finances, and everything else that pertains to your life.

God is not a slave driver. The world around us right now wants believers to think the ways of God are too hard or too limiting. That is crazy! As I mentioned earlier, in Matthew 11:29-30 Jesus definitively says that the ways of God are actually easy. Easy...if we are willing to surrender and trust.

THRIVING IN SURRENDER

You may not see an obvious correlation between surrender and thriving. The world we live in paints a picture of thriving that is based on doing whatever feels most right at any given moment. The narrative of our culture sounds something like this: "Want to eat only nuts and bananas for the rest of your life? Great! You do you, baby."

While I do support our God-given right to choose for ourselves how we want to live, I cannot support the idea that all ways lead to happiness. They just don't. Only Jesus and His way is the easy way. Ironically, it's the hardest way to embrace initially.

Yes, the way of Jesus is narrow. It is particular. You will have to let some things go as you surrender. Not all of your thoughts can stay in your brain if you want to thrive in the Lord. You will have to let Him define the narrative of your mind and your life. BUT where the world gets it wrong is they cannot understand the freedom that is found on that narrow, particularly specific way. Amazingly, God's way actually brings freedom.

We are actually called into a lifestyle of partnership with God. He doesn't need us but He likes to include us. It's just like when a parent lets a child help make a batch of cookies. The process will certainly be more messy and slower with the child involved but it brings so much joy to the parent.

Peace comes when the lines of submission are drawn. We trust Him. We let Him be the Lord and the ultimate authority of our lives. He draws us in and we learn from Him. The more we learn from Him and how He runs things, the more we are drawn in. As He draws us in He begins to trust us and He invites us to partner with Him to fulfill the dreams we now share together.

Can you see now why trust and surrender are essential to learning to love your life? He knows us even better than we know ourselves. He sees the entire timeline of our lives. He truly has our best interests in mind. In the same way we need to build trust with the Lord He builds trust with us as well.

Don't get me wrong. We are all loved the same. It is not a matter of one person being more special or more important than another. It is the reality that deep trust is a two-way street. Sometimes we want God to entrust us with something we know would bring us so much joy but we are not willing to surrender to His process. Ironically, it is often that process that He uses to prepares us to steward the blessing we have been asking for.

Think of the ways of God as the instructions a master gives to his household. Now consider how those instructions might differ from a son to a servant. The servant is given tasks and directions. The servant's only job is to complete the tasks as they are given.

The master cannot truly trust the servant if he is only willing to complete the tasks and not willing to learn why the tasks are important in the first place. A servant can have success in completing tasks while simultaneously keeping himself at a distance relationally.

The son, however, wants to spend time with the master. The master also gives the son tasks to complete to help the household run smoothly. The son completes them but he also wants to understand why the tasks are needed in the first place.

There is a transfer of understanding that takes place in the relationship between the master and the son. Even if the son does not fully understand the importance of the tasks, he is willing to learn. He understands there is intentionality at work here. As the son begins to think like the master, the son can be entrusted with more freedom and more responsibility. The master can trust the son to further his work because the son now thinks like the master.

So many of us want the freedom of a son but we don't want to learn the ways of the master. We want to have the authority and the resources of the son, but we don't want to yield to the thought processes that the master holds dear. God designed the world and He knows best how to live in it. Why would we continue to doubt His process? Why do we continue to struggle to yield to His ways?

I get it and I've been there. While I can't speak for you, my issue was always in the trust department. Can I trust God to help me renew my mind? Will it be worth it if I do? Can I trust God with my pain? Will He meet me and truly comfort me? Can I trust God with the timing of my life? Will He forget about me as I serve Him in an area that feels so far from what I really want to do with my life?

In this day and age it is more important than ever to know God's heart. There is motivational content everywhere. Every time I get on Facebook someone is telling me how I can go after my dreams, live my best life, thrive, and also not care at all about what other people think about me.

This sounds alluring for sure. What I cannot seem to understand though, is how they expect these outcomes to happen apart from true trust and surrender to the ways of God found in Christ Jesus. Nothing else will stand eternal. Maybe King David said it best:

> *"This God—his way is perfect; the word of the LORD proves true; he is a shield for all those who take refuge in him."*
> *(Psalm 18:30 ESV)*

There is no other way that is perfect but God's way. There is no other way that will prove true in the end but His. That should be a truly inspiring thought. It should conjure up incredible motivation within us! As we follow the Lord we are following THE best way for our life. His way is not being hidden from us where we never find it. It is hiding right out in the open as we decide whether or not we want to surrender to the invitation of God:

> *"You will seek me and find me, when you seek me with all your heart."*
> *(Jeremiah 29:13 ESV)*

Seek after Him, build trust, and surrender to His way. That is where you will find what you are looking for.

chapter eleven

THE UNFAIR ADVANTAGE

Change takes time. Growth is not always immediate. I know I have already mentioned that in these pages but it is important to keep reminding yourself that patience plays a role in your transformation. For me, the journey of getting out of the mess of my life has been a winding road of ups and downs which I can trace back to a prophetic dream I had at 17 years old. The theme of the dream was that Jesus wanted to be Lord of my life.

By Lord I mean He wanted me to give Him control. He wanted to take the reins of my life and truly lead me. I was saved and had been for as long as I could remember. I was doing my best to follow Him but I was conflicted in my heart. I wanted the life I wanted and I also wanted Him to be Lord. Those two things do not always go together. In the dream I realized my best efforts would not be good enough. After many days of contemplation I decided to surrender completely to Jesus. The funny thing is that I thought I already had.

Since that day at 17 I have had this same experience many times over. On the road of life I find myself having to surrender all over again, often feeling like I never really knew surrender before that moment. I began to learn that this is how He leads us.

As we say yes to Him, He takes the reins of our life. He leads, we obey, and we find ourselves learning and growing. That learning will often, in time, lead to a moment where more surrender is required to continue the journey. This is what it looks like to build trust with the Lord.

We need to train ourselves to fix our eyes on Him. We must continually look for what God is doing in our lives and focus on that. When we look at the troubles, the frustrations or the sharp left turns in the road we can get stuck. We need to train ourselves to look for Jesus because it is not our natural response to difficulty.

PITY PARTY PROM QUEEN

There are seasons of my life where I was really campaigning for the title of Pity Party Prom Queen. You know, the whole "woe is me, nothing ever goes my way" campaign slogan. Self pity is dangerous. It is a truly limiting perspective that only exists to feed insecurity and hurt. Self pity reaches out for any kind of sympathy it can find, even if it is coerced or fake. Self pity softly whispers its melancholy tale into your ears: "Just feed me. Make me feel better about myself for a moment. Fix me. Rescue me. Oh, you won't? I figured you'd say that. No one ever really wants to help me."

Why is self pity so dangerous? Because it wants to artificially feed your need and make the immediate empty feeling go away, but it never actually addresses the root of your emptiness. Understandably, there are reasons that you are needy.

We all are shaped by life circumstances. Especially in our childhood and adolescent years. God entrusted you to your parents to look after you, shape you, and help you have your needs met. For some of you, your parents were found to be untrustworthy with the precious gift that you are.

That does not mean there is something wrong with you. It means they struggled to navigate the responsibility of parenting well. I find many of us want to keep blaming our parents for things they did or didn't do that left lasting negative effects on us. Honestly, at some point we have to choose to forgive them, let them off the hook for not being a trustworthy vessel to raise one of God's precious children, and figure out how to address the collateral damage.

This may seem like an insincere approach to your issues. That is not at all my heart. But if we want to move forward we have to stop blaming and start fixing our eyes on Jesus who can actually address our issues. Remember how I said self pity wants to feed its need artificially? Jesus truly has the antidote to your pain. He wants to fill the need in your sole and heal it so it is no longer there. Self pity is dangerous because it makes us momentarily think the need is filled so we don't turn to Jesus and let Him heal it.

Living our life with Jesus as our Lord and Master does not come with an immunity card. It does not mean troubles will not come and it does not keep heart ache away. What it does provide, however, is an unfair advantage. It gives us an upper hand against the darkness that tries to shut us down. What is that advantage? It is perspective and power.

There are no forces or powers more powerful than Him. Father God and Jesus are working in completely perfect unity with Holy Spirit to bring you into your grander purposes in life. One of the best ways I can articulate this is to tell you about an encounter with Jesus I had a few years ago that deeply impacted me.

I was attending a ministry conference when I was overwhelmed by the Holy Spirit at the end of one of the sessions. I made my way to the front area for prayer and it is hard to describe what happened next. As I laid there on the floor I was taken into a vision. It was the kind of encounter where you lose all sense of anything else happening in the room.

In the vision I saw Jesus come and stand next to me and a large projector screen was in front of us. He was dressed in full regalia. He was wearing a beautiful kingly robe and crown, and He stood tall with a strong and majestic posture.

He stood next to me as I watched my life play across

this movie screen. There were images of me in my mother's womb, as an infant, a toddler, a child, etc… As each of these moments appeared on the screen it was as if Jesus was judging and then justifying each one. Most of what I saw were the painful moments of my life. He was declaring as King what He thought about these moments. How they grieved and angered Him.

What I was bearing witness to was something I had never experienced before. This was King Jesus pronouncing judgment. Not on any people but on the actions themselves. As each scene ended He somehow seemed to reconcile it, pronounce His goodness onto it, and seal it with closure.

It did something in my soul to experience Him doing that. There were no more questions about what God thought about those moments of my life. Moments of abuse. Moments of rejection. Moments of neglect. Moments of heartache. They all passed before Him as He issued His judgments with a nod of His head.

Physically, I was weeping under the intensity of the power radiating from Jesus. In the vision, I was simply stunned. I was struck by the power of our God, the supreme authority He holds, and the tender intensity that is who He is. I could feel my soul changing as the movie reel continued to show my moments. The moment where my son died. The moment of my surgeries. Then it caught up to the present day and it stopped playing.

When the images ended the encounter changed immediately. I was now sitting at an enormous table in the vision. Imagine a small lego man at a dining room table. The table was larger than I could grasp as I was positioned in the middle seat. Things were being arranged on the table like foods and plates. The table was being prepared before me.

Behind me was my Father God. He was much, much larger than me. In the distance in front of the table was a small army of demons. They were scrambling trying to come up with new ideas to hurt me, stop me, and slow me down.

Then I heard my Father God laughing. It was a deep belly laugh and He was really amused. He was laughing at their plans. He placed His hand on my shoulder and leaned down to speak in my ear.

Through His laughter He managed to say, "Look at how hard they are trying to stop you. When you are with me in heaven we will laugh for years at all their futile attempts to stop my plans for your life."

This encounter went on for the better part of an hour. I was weeping and then laughing, only to find myself weeping again under the power of God. Going into that conference I was thriving. I had come into a place of healing from many of my hurts and heartaches.

This was different. I left that encounter with a perspective that held power. There was a closure and yet a beginning in that moment. I was truly aware of the unfair advantage we all have through Jesus.

I share this moment with you because there is power in the reality of King Jesus wanting to right the wrongs in your life. There is so much power in the truth of the bigness of God and His immense power over the threats of the enemy against you. I do not believe this encounter was unique to me. This is what God is doing for you as well. He is laughing in the face of your enemies. He is preparing a table for you where you and He will laugh at the enemy's ridiculous attempts to stop you.

WHEN GOD LAUGHS

You have truly been given an unfair advantage. God is holding all the keys. The breakthrough. The healing. The perspective. The power. It's time to do something about that. It's time to let go of the things that hold you back and run right into His welcoming embrace. Can you trust Him enough to lean in when you want to lean away? Can you see how it really is the enemy throwing these hurdles of doubt, disappointment, and disillusionment at you?

Don't waste another moment thinking the enemy has the upper hand in your life. The demons that want to stop you are so small and so powerless compared to Jesus. Anything small can appear big if you focus on it enough. The opposition against you can feel insurmountable if that is all you are willing to acknowledge.

The sound of God laughing has stayed with me. I hear it from time to time in my memory. It is a great reminder that God is infinitely bigger than any problems I am facing. I find so much comfort in that. Not that He always fixes my problems, because that is certainly not true. It's just that He is with me, and that is truly enough.

When we lean in and embrace this unfair advantage we rise above the struggles of this life. Take heart today. There may be a war of emotions and circumstances around you but Jesus is stronger. You may be facing some really hard things but you are not alone. God is with you.

I want to remind you that thriving doesn't mean you will never stumble or struggle. I am not advocating perfection here. That's why these tools are helpful because you will probably need to use them more than once. There will be traps and snares laid for you by the enemy and there will be days you step in them.

Thriving is not the same thing as arriving at a place where no sin or struggle exists. It simply means that when you do struggle, you will know where to go and what to do so you don't stay in the struggle. You have the ability to see Jesus regardless of what is going on around you.

What would your life look like if you had resolve and closure from the biggest moments of hurt you have experienced? Can you identity a theme to those pains? Maybe it is rejection, abandonment, fear, or worry. When we can own and be honest about our hurts we can get them healed so much faster. Denial never helped anybody. Identify those hurdles and call them out as distractors.

REMOVE THE LIES IN YOUR WAY

One way to do this is to journal out a list of lies you are currently believing. Sounds intense, I know. But think of it as cleaning out a cluttered closet. Sometimes we don't even know what our hurdles are until we put them on paper.

In the 1970s the FBI began a study that evolved into the tactical approach in hostage negotiation. They focused on high intensity situations and uncovered a simple yet profoundly impactful discovery. They discovered that negative emotions rattle around in our minds at least 3 times more intensely than any other emotion.

That means your fear, anger, hate, and other negative emotions will feel more intense than anything else. This study led to another startling conclusion. The simple act of acknowledging that negative emotion has the power to release that intensity 100% of the time.

That means the ultra basic act of labeling how you are feeling can immediately release the intensity attached to it. You have the power to alleviate some of the tension you feel simply by being willing to acknowledge and identify it. Your brain wants to help you and you can help your brain do that. Don't bottle up negativity. Don't ignore it or stuff it.

Every so often I list the lies I am believing in my journal. I don't exactly look forward to these days but I love them anyway. I want to know what I am dealing with. I want to know the ways the enemy is working on me. I want to know what is lurking beneath the negativity I may feel because our negativity is usually fueled by the subtle lies we believe.

Getting off track with the Lord is actually a fairly subtle process. Lies can stack up in your mind without you even realizing it. I like to confront this head on by routinely looking at what is going on in my thoughts. If I do not take the time to assess what I am believing those beliefs will just linger in my subconscious directing my life in a way I did not necessarily want to go.

My process for this is pretty simple. I grab my journal

and some time alone. I pray a simple prayer asking the Lord to shine His revealing light in my heart. King David prayed it best:

> *"Search me [thoroughly], O God, and know my heart; Test me and know my anxious thoughts; And see if there is any wicked or hurtful way in me, And lead me in the everlasting way." (Psalm 139:23-24 AMP)*

Then I write "Lies I am Believing" and make a numerical list as they come to mind. They are usually about one sentence long.

Some examples would be:

1. That people don't like being my friend.
2. That God does not want to help me with this problem.
3. That I don't know how to hear God's voice.

After I have written all the lies I can think of I go back and ask the Lord for His truth about that lie. I make a divine exchange of sorts. I give Him my wrong thinking and I take His thoughts as my own. It is like a divine exchange that begins with my recognition of which thoughts and beliefs need to get out of me. I mark out the life and write the truth. If there is room I will write it on the same line.

~~1. That people don't like being my friend.~~
TRUTH: I have great friends who accept me as I am.
~~2. That God does not want to help me.~~
TRUTH: The solution I need is already in the works!
~~3. That I don't know how to hear God's voice.~~
TRUTH: I do hear God. He is working on my confidence.

There are days where I have filled a whole journal page with lies I am believing. There is no shame in that. Lies lose their power when they are brought into the light. As science has shown, you will feel relief just acknowledging that they are there. You have the upper hand here. It is your brain.

You get to decide what stays and what goes. Even if it is a struggle to believe the truth it is a struggle you can fight and win. Why? Because you have an unfair advantage. The Prince of Peace is in you. His purposes will not fail. Your partnership with Him is enough to vanquish every lie you are believing.

Set aside some time with Jesus soon. Give Him an opportunity to talk to you about the moments of hurt you have experienced. Be sure to write down what you hear the Lord saying so you can remember. Then take some time to list out any lies that may be hiding in you. There is no reason to be afraid. I am praying you find these tools helpful for you.

Father God, thank you for this process. It is so hard to open our hurt up to you but we know you are with us. We know you can help us. Bring your peace over us right now. Let your love be felt tangibly. I pray over this process that you would shine a light on every lie hiding right now. Speak your truths into these lies. Help us to hear from you clearly. Amen.

chapter twelve

PERMISSION TO THRIVE

Sometime during the worst time of my life I had an epiphany. It was simple yet so earth shattering. This is *my* life. Sounds revolutionary don't you think? I realized no one but Jesus will truly know what it's like to be me. What I need. How I think. Who I want to become. Why I am the way I am. And because no one will truly understand these things there is no one standing in the way of my thriving but me.

I had mistakenly believed for many years that it was Jesus standing in my way. That sounds intense, but think about it. All those beliefs about how God thinks, feels, and acts toward you are a part of your theological outlook. Do you believe He is far off? Indifferent? Do you believe God is deeply in love with just about everyone but you? That He prefers to favor other people and leave you to do the hard work? If you resonate with any thoughts like those than you probably think Jesus is standing in your way too. Spoiler Alert: He is not the reason you struggle.

After fixing my theology and encountering the amazing love of God, I realized the only force left that was powerful enough to stop the flow of God in my life was me. I was the reason I wasn't thriving. I was afraid to make the changes I so badly needed to make. I was too afraid of what might happen if I tried. I am forever thankful that I finally did get the courage to embrace the real me. It began in the months following the counseling retreat in Louisiana that I mentioned in chapter one.

THE MOST INCREDIBLE BREAKTHROUGH

During one of the sessions with the counselor, my husband Grant and I were both given a paper with a story and a description on it. The instructions were clear. Read it and don't talk about it to each other. "Read and find yourself in the story," the counselor said. "There is no wrong answer." As a former control freak who had not yet been set free, I immediately disregarded his instruction and started scanning the pages to find which of the characters appeared to be the "right" answer.

The story was of a married couple at the birth of their first child. The new mom, having just had her first baby placed onto her chest, cradles the baby and is overwhelmed with emotion. "Isn't this the best day of our lives?!?" she says as she looks lovingly at her husband.

The husband is still in a stunned state of shock from just witnessing the gore of birth for the first time. He simply mutters, smiling, "Uh, yeah," as he tries to process all that just occurred.

The wife sinks into herself and begins to feel that she was wrong. This was obviously not the amazing moment she had thought they were sharing. Maybe they were not as connected as she had felt. Her mind begins to race as it spirals into subtle sadness.

I read the story and the description accompanying it. Words about being a self-validated person vs. an others-validated person. Essentially a self-validated person does not need external confirmation to feel what they feel. Their feelings just are what they are and they acknowledge them as that. Others-validated people validate their feelings by external means. A feeling of joy can turn off if others around them don't share that feeling of joy or validate that it is a good feeling to have in that situation.

My mind went into deadlock. I honestly could not tell which was the better answer and therefore could not admit which person I thought I was in the story. I saw myself so clearly in the others-validated camp and yet I was determined to not believe that indicated a problem. Hilariously, I was searching everywhere in the story for validation that my assessment was not only accurate but the preferred option.

As the counselor came back in the room for a discussion I was faced with the reality that I was, in fact, an others-validated person. I say "was" because miraculously I no longer am. A miracle began to take place in that session that took about two years to come to fruition. I began to realize that I have the ability to feel as I feel…even if no one else shares that feeling. This is particularly hard in marriage.

Women are so interconnected. A bad day with the kids often becomes a bad day all around. A hurtful situation at work often spills over into the home. We want to feel collectively too. We feel so overcome with love for our husband and we want to know he is feeling that same feeling in that same moment. If he isn't, it is like a crushing blow that often causes us to rethink the strength of our love altogether.

This is where my breakthrough came. I stopped rethinking what I felt and I simply owned it. Feeling overjoyed at an amazing night with friends? Great! You can express that and not need someone else to concur. Processing heartache because your favorite TV drama killed off your favorite character? Great! You don't have to feel stupid that you have feelings. You don't have to feel bad that you are having an emotional reaction to life. And you don't have to apologize for it.

For me, attacking the others-validated framework was an intentional deep dive. I didn't work on this because I felt that I was bad or flawed. I did it because I realized there was hope that I would not have to live my life being tossed about on the waves of other people's opinions. I got a vision for what Valentine's Day or Christmas would be like if I wasn't so insecure. I got hungry for a life where I could thrive and I went all in.

Others-validated people don't have the confidence to feel for themselves. We often don't have the skills to navigate our feelings when they differ from the popular opinion so we shut them down. No one wants to be the odd one out, right? This mind-set also struggles to own any emotions that are positive for fear that they are not really real. Ironically, our negativity doesn't seem to need validation. At least, not as much.

That means others-validated people are mostly missing out on the good parts of life. The beautiful thing happening right now in this moment is that your brain is capable of being retrained. Your mind can be renewed and you can learn new skills. In the same way we learn basic reading and writing we can learn emotional intelligence as well.

I got such a hunger for breakthrough in this. I can't count how many times I would be elated about something only to see my husband not sharing that feeling. It would crush me and suck out my joy.

The sad part is that he is simply an even keeled person but I had put a soul crushing gavel in his hand by giving him the place of validator of my feelings. That was an unfair thing to do to him. I got excited about taking that imaginary gavel out of his hand and throwing it away.

On our drive home from that retreat we had a good conversation. I admitted I did not want to live this way anymore but I had no idea if I could change. My entire life could be summed up in the others-validated category and I felt like I was now flying blind. How would it feel to feel in this new way? Would it even feel like feeling at all? Full disclosure, by the end of that conversation it had become an argument as I was still unsatisfied with his response to my desire to change. He wasn't matching my level of excitement that this would be good for me. It was yet another example of why this issue needed to go.

I made a commitment in that argument. It was probably more of a declaration or manifesto. From this point forward, I declared, I will admit and confess every time I am reaching for someone to validate my feelings. I realized I would not be able to do this alone so I roped in my husband and a few close friends.

For months I was true to my word. I would stop him in the middle of a sentence and share that I could feel myself reaching and trying to be validated by his approval of me. I would share with him and my closest friends as this was happening.

After a month or so I felt pretty stupid. My confession was not any less frequent and the feelings inside myself were not changing as obviously as I had hoped. I would sit awkwardly trying to assure myself that it was ok no one was feeling like me. It did not feel good but I didn't give up.

There are so many things in life that require grind and hustle. We set a goal and then we put our head down and do the hard things. Keep showing up, keep working, keep doing the things in hopes that it will pay off.

We don't stop to count the fruit of our labor every day because we know it will take time. Building a business, getting a degree, parenting, and so many other areas of life require this. So does our personal development. Change takes time…a lot of time.

Making this kind of change is no easy feat. So many of us give up because we can't see immediate fruit from the first week of our hard work. Don't let that be you. I was confessing not because I believed being others-validated was a sin, but because I wanted to call it out. I wanted to tell my brain and myself that this was not the way I wanted to be wired anymore. God did not make me to be so affected by those around me and I no longer wanted that for myself.

About 8 months into this journey I had a breakthrough. By then, I was not confessing and proclaiming as much because my new pattern was to recognize that reaching feeling and put it in check with more ease than ever before. I could tell I was changing. It was amazing and so peaceful.

Around this time it was Grant's birthday and I had planned a little dinner party for him. A lot of thought had gone into that night to make it special. I wanted him to feel so loved and celebrated.

As we drove home from the restaurant I asked him, "Did you have fun tonight?" It was a loaded question. I didn't want to know if he only had fun. I wanted to know if he felt loved, known, enjoyed himself, liked his presents, and so many other things. Without taking his eyes off the road he said in a calm tone with no inflection, "Yeah."

A few minutes of driving passed by and it hit me like a lighting bolt. His answer had not affected me at all. I had not second guessed myself, told myself I should have picked a different venue, or gone into a downward spiral of disappointment because he had not started raving that it was the best night of his life.

I nearly jumped out of my skin at that realization and I blurted out "OH MY GOSH!!! I just realized I don't even care how you responded to my question!!!" We had a little celebration of my progress that night and I have never been the same since. Of course I cared that he answered yes, but I didn't care how he answered with yes. It was thrilling and empowering. Yes, there was more breakthrough and healing that would come, but this was the turning point.

Letting go of an others-validated mentality is not the same thing as becoming indifferent or detached from what people think. It simply means you don't structure your life around the validation of other people.

I am not suggesting you do not need people in your life as godly counsel. We all need mentors. We need spiritual mothers and fathers to help us see the things we might be blind to. However, even these relationships should point you to Jesus. They should point you to establishing a life where you are following Holy Spirit's leading, not just the instruction of a mentor.

Why do you need to be self-validated? Because Jesus is in you and He is leading you. Other people may not see that leading at times. We cannot live our lives based on the validation of others because other people are not our Creator. You were created intentionally, purposefully, and for a unique plan. Accomplishing that plan will require you to trust the leadership of Jesus in your life above every other voice you hear.

Insecurities take many shapes and forms. For so many

of us, we are waiting for someone to give us permission to overcome them. What are you actually waiting for? For someone else to think you are flawed and shame you into making a change? Are you waiting to be coerced by the people around you because they just can't put up with you anymore? I sincerely hope that is not why you are waiting.

I think you are waiting for permission because you have not found a better vision for your life. You haven't tasted the freedom that is awaiting you. Listen, if you are waiting for a green light, you have it. This book is your permission. This book exists because I know there are others like me out there. There are women and men who are living as a lesser version of themselves because they haven't seen the better version yet.

GREEN LIGHT, BABY, GREEN LIGHT!

You are empowered by Jesus Himself to wake up and take action, put your head down, and grind. It is time to lay aside the distractions of other people's opinions. It is time to focus on Him and that abundant life He promised you in John 10:10.

Did you know that verse is more accurately translated to have life and a life better than anyone else? What does a life better than anyone else look like to you? I'm not talking nicer cars, better clothes, or fancier houses. Think about what a life better than anyone else looks like on the inside.

Very few people are walking around truly at peace with themselves, feeling satisfied with the life they are living, and experiencing joy just because it's there to feel. Jesus has invited you into a life with Him where you are thriving and you feel it. It's possible. Actually, it's probable.

There is nothing more powerful than Jesus except you. Technically you are not more powerful than Jesus but you've been given the free will ability to choose the direction for your life. God honors your will so much that He will let you stand in your own way if you want to.

That is a sobering thought but it is the truth. It is time to get out of your own way. Flush your doubts down the toilet and get ready to do the hard work of believing in yourself. All of heaven is cheering you on!

You may not have anyone in your life that truly believes in you but the book of Hebrews says that you have a great cloud of witnesses that are cheering you on from heaven. I believe in you. Jesus believes in you. Father God is elated at the idea of showing you how to be the truest version of yourself. Holy Spirit has made himself available to you to equip you to overcome whatever else might stand in your way. So, what are you waiting for?

Don't make a change because someone else wants you to or because someone else thinks you should. Do it for yourself. Dare to dream that your life could become something you truly love. Risk hoping that you are strong enough to persevere as you recategorize the subconscious thoughts that have you on an auto pilot mode of mediocrity.

Here's the honest truth: you can thrive. You can fall in love with your life and stay in love with your life. Is it hard? For sure. Is it worth it? No question. The permission you have been waiting for has been sitting within you all along.

Jesus already gave you the green light to freedom and abundance. Now it's time for you to give it to yourself. As you do you too will get out of it because you learned to love it.

About the author

Hi! I'm Rachel. By now you know quite a lot about my life already. Since I know some of you are borderline stalkers (I mean curious people) I will go ahead and fill in some details. I was born and raised in Springfield, Missouri, home of the cashew chicken dinner. I was a below average athlete (I still am) and an above average dreamer.

I graduated from Baylor University in 2005. A time I like to call "pre-Joanna Gaines" when Waco was not the wonderland it is today. To me, however, it will always be home. In addition to learning just how glorious fried chicken can be, Waco taught me to love the local church. So much so that I have been a part of planting churches ever since.

I met my husband Grant, got married, had my first child, bought my first home, and so many other precious memories all while living in Waco. Before we were truly ready to say goodbye God called us to Norman, Oklahoma to help plant a church as the youth pastors.

Our time in Norman was transformative and magical,

although it was the backdrop for most of the stories in this book. After about four years God laid it on our hearts to move to Oklahoma City to plant another church. With a pocket full of promises and a lot of naiveté we headed to our new home in the fall of 2013.

Our time planting and pastoring Bethel OKC has been the greatest time of our lives. We have had front row seats to watching God do some pretty unbelievable things in our midst!

A few years into our journey with Bethel OKC God asked us to have another baby. It will forever be one of the hardest yes' I have ever given the Lord. A little over a year later Grace Pearl Wortman was born in December of 2016. She is truly my pearl of great price. The fruit of choosing faith over fear. My ever constant reminder that God's grace is with us in every season.

Let's get connected!

www.rachelwortman.com
The Art Of Being You podcast
Facebook & Instagram @rachelwortman

Freebies

I LOVE gifts and free stuff so I am sharing that love with you! Head over to www.rachelwortman.com and check out our "Freebies" tab for some follow up material to help you on your journey.

Made in the USA
Monee, IL
27 November 2021